FINDING EACH OTHER

Mary Olsen Kelly
and Don Kelly

A Fireside Book
Published by Simon & Schuster
New York • London • Toronto
Sydney • Tokyo • Singapore

FIRESIDE
Simon & Schuster Building
Rockefeller Center
1230 Avenue of the Americas
New York, New York 10020

FIRESIDE and colophon are registered trademarks
of Simon & Schuster Inc.

Designed by Liney Li
Manufactured in the United States of America

10   9   8   7   6   5   4   3   2   1

Library of Congress Cataloging in Publication Data

Kelly, Mary Olsen.
Finding each other / Mary Olsen Kelly and Don Kelly.
p.   cm.
1. Love.   2. Interpersonal relations.   3. Mate selection.   4. Self-
actualization (Psychology)   I. Kelly, Don,   II. Title.
HQ801.K45   1992
646.7'7—dc20   91-36033
CIP

ISBN: 0-671-72635-8

CONTENTS

ACKNOWLEDGMENTS

We are blessed to have incredibly loving families and friends who have created beauty and love in our lives; thank you for all your support. Ole and Joyce, Ivie and Jack, Bow and Chuck, Bob and Donna, Janet and Al, Joan and Ed, Vicki and Steve, Winifred and Virgil, Barbara and Sam, Arne and Ann, Helen and Tom, Diana and Ted, Serge and Gloria, Karen and Don, Peggy and Fred, Jan and Richard, Kevin and Drea, Robert and Rachel, Heidi and Scott, Pam and Steve, Sanford and Chris, Bobbi and Larry, Frank and Barb, Harry and Minnie, Tim and Sheila, Sune and Emily; thank you for finding each other. You are role models for the power of loving partnership.

Thank you to Barbara Gess, our editor and friend, for helping this book through its quantum leaps. Thanks to all the wonderful people who have taken our workshops, heard us speak, bought our books, and supported us as teachers. Thank you to Dr. Peggy Bassett for being a courageous beacon of light and wisdom to us.

E ALOHA PAOLE
May Our Love Be Ever-lasting
(Hawaiian blessing)

INTRODUCTION
Welcome to the Journey

This book is for everyone who wants more love, happiness, and self-understanding in their lives. It offers a double benefit: the opportunity to attract your ideal life mate as well as your own personal growth.

We have had the pleasure of observing a wonderful phenomenon in the past decade. A new kind of love is emerging, a love that is both deep, spiritual, and committed at the same time that it is spontaneous and fresh. Postmodern, post-feminist, and post–New Age, this new form of love integrates all the learning of the past decades into a deeper, more conscious and caring commitment.

The best news of all is that a new kind of partnership based on this love is available to those who choose it. We have come across remarkable couples who demonstrate this new partnership. We have watched them, interviewed them, and asked them to talk about their relationship and how they found each other.

We call this new kind of loving relationship "ideal life mates."

In talking with these couples, we found certain feelings and phrases recurring frequently. These feelings are the ones you will be looking for, and finding, as you go through the program in this book and connect with your true life mate. Life-mate couples speak of "recognizing each other," they feel that by finding each other they have "come home." Sometimes they refer to each other as "the one I've been looking for all my life" and "the man or woman of my dreams" or "my soul mate."

You have probably heard about soul mates at some point in your romantic research. Soul mates are partners who are bound by a karmic link that causes them to reincarnate to experience love together and spiritually evolve together.

We are more concerned with this life rather than past lives—couples that find each other *now* to love each other at this time in history. We have chosen in our work to focus on love relationships that are designed to be fully realized in this lifetime. We call these relationships "life mates" because they are specifically focused on growth and achievements in this current life.

There are many books about relationships, and even a few about how to find your perfect mate. We have found that most of these books concentrate on the *exterior* aspects of this search. They offer tips on where to find eligible men, how to write an effective personal ad, and which supermarket to shop in to meet a lover.

We are concerned more with the *internal* elements—what is going on inside you. We have found that it is the mental focus, the emotional and spiritual energy you carry inside you, and the ways you work with this energy, that magnetizes and attracts your perfect life mate to you.

We believe that human beings act as a mirror to reflect back to others the qualities that exist in themselves. In this book, we share techniques for clearing the mirror and consciously creating the person you want to be in a relationship, so that you mirror and attract your appropriate partner. We explain the main steps to finding each other and share many concepts and exercises with you. You will learn how to heal and release past relationships, how to become the most fully complete and loving version of *you*, so that you can move ahead to a more loving and fulfilling partnership.

This book is geared to people who are truly ready to experience the fulfillment of a loving partnership, and who are not afraid to do the work that it takes to attract someone of value. Perhaps there is only one ideal life mate for you on this earth, or perhaps there is a cluster of partners that can mirror and reflect your deepest true love. We believe there is *at least* one person. In this book we share the attitudes, practices, and self-healing techniques that can help you prepare yourself for the eminent arrival of your ideal life mate.

"When the student is ready, the master will appear" is a well-known phrase to spiritual seekers. We paraphrase the same concept as "When the lover is whole and complete, the life mate will appear."

We believe that it is never too late to find love in your life. In fact, we found each other after many years of actively searching for our ideal love partner, through several marriages and other happy and not-so-happy relationships. We eventually found each other by using the tools and techniques shared in this book.

We have experienced long-term love relationships that were no longer fulfilling, and have experienced letting go of the old to let the new shine in. We learned about relationships "the hard way"—by doing what *doesn't* work. In the process of finding each other, we have discovered what *does* work.

So we offer maps of the terrain ahead. Don't think of us as experts, but rather as guides on an emotional safari through the jungle of romance and relationships. We have journeyed ahead and have discovered some paths you can take to avoid the swamps and bogs. We have also used our machetes to carve out a few shortcuts to the night-blooming jasmine and the rainbow waterfalls.

The maps in this guidebook can save you years of discovering "the hard way," and can allow you to reach your goal of an ideal life mate much more efficiently.

We have developed a set of basic principles that informs all our workshops, and that guides the healing and counseling work we do.

Here they are:

1. Replace fear with love.

2. If you want more love, *give* more love.

3. Choose to forgive yourself and others.

4. Connect with your Higher Self on a daily basis.

5. Bring your highest and best self to the relationship.

6. Clear the mirror, heal, forgive, release, and complete.

7. Take back your power and move forward in love.

8. Expect the best because you deserve the best: What if it works?

9. We each have an important life purpose as an individual.

10. We have a shared life purpose as a couple.

11. Bless the present, trust your Higher Self, expect the best that life has to offer.

12. Become your best self and your ideal life mate will appear.

13. Become whom you seek to attract.

As you can see, these guidelines are targeted to single people who are really ready to meet their ideal life mate. They outline some of the important polishing touches that help you increase your chances of success in this emotional journey toward partnership.

It is an adventure and a journey—one with many dangers and many rewards. It requires you to look into the mirror of your own soul, to take stock of who you have been in your past relationships and who you can be in your future partnership.

Why do you need to work on yourself? Why do you have to do all this work just to meet the love of your life?

Because, if you keep doing things the way you have been, you will continue to get the same results. If you are single and you honestly want to create a loving relationship in your life, you are obviously going to have to change.

"If it's not broke, don't fix it." That means, if you are happy being single and you don't want to change, that's fine. But if you do want to get new results in your life, or if you aren't getting the results you want, you have to change something you are doing.

Maybe you're thinking, "But why do *I* have to change? Why can't *he* or *she* change, or men or women, as a sex, change? Why does it always have to be *me*?"

Because you are the only one who *can* change. We can't change anyone else. We can't change men or women as a whole. Ultimately, the power must come from within each one of us. We have only one power and that is our ability to change ourselves—to grow, improve, and excel. We have the opportunity to work on the areas of our lives that aren't giving us the satisfaction we long for. We can only change ourselves, so that's where we must start.

The good news is that it's worth it. The beauty, love, romance, and joy of a happy partnership are enormous rewards waiting for you at the end of the tunnel. It is definitely worth the effort. Ask any happy couple if the agony of their previous relationships and the learning they gained haven't been dwarfed by the joy of their current happy relationship.

You will meet many of these kindred souls throughout the book as we share the stories of life mates finding each other. These are stories of success and stories of challenges, such as:

- Georgia, a 42-year-old woman who had never been married, and wondered if she was just too independent and strong-willed to ever find a mate. Until she found him.

- Sherrie, a 39-year-old woman who healed herself from a horribly painful divorce, and after three years rebuilt her self-esteem to the point where she was happy with herself and her life. She met her current husband within weeks after realizing that she could go out alone, do things by herself, and be happy as a single woman, if necessary, for the rest of her life.

- Paul, a 45-year-old man in a fourteen-year marriage who knew that the love, passion, and romance was long gone from his relationship. He had the courage to change his life, rebuild himself, and attract the love of his dreams.

- Sophia, a 54-year-old widow with five grown children, who decided she didn't want to spend the rest of her life alone. She got into a position where she could meet hundreds of eligible men and found her new life mate.

- Debbie, 37, survivor of two divorces, knew that she had a lot of work to do on herself to avoid attracting another disaster. She committed to this program. At the end of a year and a half, she had broken through past patterns, learned a tremendous amount about herself, and increased her self-worth. She knew she deserved to be loved by the way she was willing to give love. She met her ideal life mate and is happily married. She feels that the first two marriages were "rehearsals" to get ready for the real thing.

- Sam, a 30-year-old man who has never been married, longs for a life mate but has set impossible standards. When he meets someone who might qualify, he is too shy to speak to her. We share with you a program for Sam that helped him discover what he really needed in a relationship, how to get comfortable with women, and how to be a little more realistic about his qualities of satisfaction.

These are a few of the people we have worked with using this program. In each case, they were ready to commit to changing themselves because they were serious about wanting to attract their ideal life mate.

Are you ready? Then let's move ahead and begin by clearing the mirror.

Part One

CLEARING THE MIRROR

■

This book is divided into two main sections. The first part, Clearing the Mirror, deals with healing past loves, discovering who you are in a relationship, and breaking old destructive patterns so you are able to bring the most whole, complete, and loving version of yourself into your life-mate relationship.

The techniques for attracting your ideal life mate are given in the second part of this book. The reason is this: if you just skip ahead to the Attracting part, you will learn some very powerful tools. You will attract many people into your life.

But until you are whole, healed, and ready to give love from a place of power and self-esteem, until you have "cleared your mirror," you will attract the same kind of relationships that you have in the past.

Many people long for a partner who will be a savior—someone to come along and magically transform their lives. This is not the way it works. You must take responsibility for creating your life, for changing the things that are not working, and for improving your confidence and self-esteem to the point that you know you deserve the best. You are worth the time and effort it takes to change, but you are the only one who can make these changes in your life.

"Clearing the mirror" means several things. It is based on the premise that we are mirrors of each other, and we reflect back to each other all the time. If you are a "clear mirror," you will attract a life mate with the same clarity as your own.

If you have dark spots and pains that cloud the mirror, you will attract a partner with the same type of clouds and issues to work through. Many times the purpose of a relationship is to help each partner clean that part of the mirror. Relationships from your past can be viewed in this way.

It takes tremendous courage to look at yourself this clearly—the courage of a warrior. To take responsibility for your life and for the relationships you have created requires some in-depth soul searching. You will not always like what you find lurking inside. Sometimes it will be confrontational and painful—that is often the nature of growth.

To break the patterns from your past and create healthy new ones, you must make changes in *yourself*. That is often the most difficult thing to do. We always want the other person to change; but no matter how it looks at the time, it is always we— you and I—who have to make the changes.

If you are seriously committed to attracting your ideal life mate, you will read every word of this book and do all the exercises. If you are only marginally committed, you will skip around, pass over important exercises, and get only mediocre results.

It is a lot of work. There are a lot of exercises here, and a lot of concepts to learn and integrate. But if you really want to change yourself and your life in order to open up and receive the love of your life, you will do it. But the process will work, to the extent that you commit to it with your heart, soul, and body.

This is a glorious adventure with a double benefit, because you are working on yourself and therefore are growing and changing. At the same time, you are getting yourself ready for your ideal life mate so that you can have a love relationship that is "the stuff of dreams."

Your loving relationship can be everything you want it to be because love is what you think it is. Your attitude about relationships and love determines the results you get. If you think that relationships are difficult, they are. If you think that dreams come true and that you deserve incredible love, you do.

If you believe that there is an ideal life mate for you somewhere across time and space, there is. We know that this is true because we see it happening all around us. We have also experienced it ourselves.

This wonderful story about the thirst and longing for wisdom also applies to the thirst for love, or spiritual evolution, or whatever you want in your life:

Socrates had a student once who asked for the secrets to wisdom. He begged his teacher for the secret keys to knowledge. Socrates took the boy by the hand and led him to a stream. Once there, he forced the boy's head under the water and held it there as the boy sputtered and gasped. He let go of the boy's head, and after the boy had regained his composure, Socrates asked, "What did you want more than anything?"

"Air," the boy answered.

"When you want knowledge as much as you wanted air, you will have it," Socrates answered.

When you want to *give* love as much as the boy wanted air, you will have it. Notice we said *give*, not *get*. If you want to *get* love all the time, it implies neediness and a lack of wholeness on your part. You will always feel needy when love comes from that intention.

When you are ready to *give* love from the endless fountain of your deep inner well of love, you will attract the love you have always dreamed of.

If you want more love, *give* more love.

Let's clear the mirror! We'll begin by healing our past loves.

◢

1.

Healing
Past Loves

If you want to achieve new results—that is, you want to attract a loving life mate—then you must change what you are doing. If you keep doing what you have done in the past, you will keep getting the same results.

When energy is being held and directed into the past, and into fears of repeating the past experiences we have associated with pain, there is very little energy for dealing with the present. For instance, if 80 percent of your energy is tied up in memories of past hurts and painful relationships, you have only 20 percent energy to commit to attracting your ideal life mate.

It takes a substantial amount of energy to cause anything to happen in this world. So you must free up the energy you will need by healing your past loves and putting them to rest. You must make room, open up the space in your heart and mind for the new to come in. The only way to do that is to clear out the old.

Why? Because "whatever you haven't learned will repeat itself until you learn it." It's like a persistent fourth-grade teacher who made you write something over and over again.

Whatever you don't want to look at in your life will continue to repeat itself until the message is so strong it smacks you between the eyes. In the same manner, you will repeat your past mistakes with relationships until you learn from them and break those old patterns.

After our workshops, participants often ask for individual counseling. Most of the people we counsel come to us for the same reason: they are still holding on to a long-lost love.

These people, in some cases, fantasized and mythologized the person in their past to the point of obsession. Even though it is obvious that the relationship is over, they cling to it in the hope of recapturing the magic that once was there.

There is no way that you will be able to attract the next major love in your life if you continue to carry this emotional baggage. It is time to let the past go and clear yourself of past attachments. If you don't, you will continue to attract people into your life who are also still attached to someone from their past.

You are the mirror; you attract the people who you are.

Debbie, 37, survivor of two divorces, knew that she had a lot of work to do on herself to avoid attracting another disastrous relationship. She committed to the program in this book for healing herself and healing her past loves.

At the end of a year and a half, Debbie had broken through past patterns and learned a tremendous amount about herself. She had increased her self-esteem and feelings of worthiness, and knew she deserved to be loved in the way she was willing to give love.

Debbie was able to see all her relationships as forwarding—moving her along a life path that was filled with growth, creativity, and love as well as some hard lessons. Once she began to see her life as one big learning experience, she realized that she had created the relationships from her past so that she could learn the very lessons they offered.

She met her ideal life mate soon after her second divorce was final, and is very happily married. Debbie feels that the first two marriages were "rehearsals" to get her ready for the real thing. She is very grateful for the lessons learned in her previous relationships, and her current marriage benefits from those lessons.

Everyone is looking for love, yet often we settle for relationships that are not really supportive or healthy simply because we want to feel love so badly. Deep inside, we long for a real connection, a feeling of unity and completion with a lover who brings balance and peace along with sensuality and companionship. Somehow in our hearts we know that such a person exists—if we could only find him or her.

Yet, many people keep falling into the same painful patterns in relationships. They repeat these patterns with each new love affair, never learning from their past mistakes, never allowing these life lessons to take hold.

Remember, if you resist something, it will persist. The more you cling to an idea, the more it repeats. Don't let your past define your future!

Once you begin to view all the relationships and experiences you've had in life in this broader context, you can see how they have taught you and molded you.

The journey of self-discovery is never-ending. The same process of growth that occurs in every cell of our bodies in every moment is also happening in our consciousness; we are constantly learning and processing new information.

Not only is the healing process essential for moving ahead and creating your ideal life mate but it can also be extremely enlightening and a lot of fun. So take the opportunity to do some rigorous self-inventory, and put together your "consciousness résumé." What kinds of therapeutic work have you done? What books have you read? What workshops and seminars have you attended? What spiritual experiences have you had?

And what areas of your life are still not working? This is a good place to find out what work needs to be done. Remember, the key to all of this is change. The circumstances in your relationships will not change until *you* do.

It may take some work to counteract the negative programming of a lifetime, so that you arrive at the state of being where you can honestly claim to deserve the best. Most of us have been warped by parental and cultural training. Our society has some cruel traps built into its very foundation, and many people have been victims of these traps.

So do whatever you can to learn and grow. Clear the blocks that you may have developed in your early parental training. The human-potential movement of the past twenty years has provided many fantastic psychologies, workshops, and trainings, and a wealth of written material you can use for personal growth. Read, learn, take these workshops, get therapy, and heal yourself. Take action. Do something to promote the healing process.

Throughout the rest of the book, we will share some Power Tools with you. Some of them are techniques or things for you to do. Some are attitudes or states of mind that, when developed, will act as powerful life-changers for you and equally powerful magnetizers to draw your ideal life mate into your life. All of these Power Tools will work magic if you use them diligently. The changes you make in yourself will have a ripple effect on your whole life, and everything around you will change, too.

◪ POWER TOOL 1

What If It Works?

We were taught from when we were little children to ask, "What is the worst thing that can happen?" We concentrate on the very worst possible scenario, and then try to decide if we will be able to deal with that worst case. We are taught to worry about a lot of worst-case scenarios that *never happen*. We are taught that life doesn't work, and so we spend a lot of time worrying, judging, criticizing, and evaluating everything in our lives.

We suggest, instead, that you begin to open up to the real possibility that life works! What if all the techniques in this book worked for you? What if you could find your ideal life mate? What if it all works?

The "What if it works?" attitude is one of optimism. It is the courage to start fresh, with an open heart and an open mind. It is having the courage to change, and to know that you deserve the best relationship for you. It is an attitude of openness, a willingness to try something new, a chance to grow and change.

The antithesis of "What if it works?" is "What if it doesn't work? What if I get my hopes up, I fall in love, it doesn't work, and I'm disappointed again? What if I open myself up, become vulnerable and giving, and it doesn't work and I'm hurt badly again?"

This is a defense mechanism that you have created to protect yourself from being hurt. It makes perfect sense to ask these questions; you are just trying to protect yourself from pain. Just make sure you are not protecting yourself from love, too.

Every relationship has an element of risk. You may attract the most wonderful life mate in the world; on the other hand, you may attract someone who isn't so wonderful. At some point, you will simply have to muster up the courage to enter another relationship regardless of the risk.

You can easily start by saying, "What if it works? What if there is an ideal life mate for me, just waiting around the corner? What if I can heal myself of past hurts and open my heart to new love? What if it works?"

When we first got together, Mary was very worried about all the ways that our new love might not work. There were lots of factors that could have stopped the relationship from flowering.

Every time Mary felt a doubt or fear creeping up, Don would say, "What if it works? What if all the awful things you are creating in your mind *don't* happen? What if it all works out?"

This was such a radical reversal of the fears she was entertaining that Mary had to just laugh out loud and accept the possibility that it might all work out just fine. Instead of saying, "This is too good to be true," she started to say, "This is good enough to be true."

◪ POWER TOOL 2

Forgive Others

The dictionary defines *forgive* as "to grant pardon without harboring resentment, to excuse for a fault or offense." Forgiveness is the most direct, effective, and powerful healing tool that exists. Forgiveness and love are the antidotes to the pain that you carry within yourself.

Forgiveness is just forgiveness. It does not imply that the other person is right! Total forgiveness means giving up all desire to punish yourself or to punish the other person.

If you do *not* forgive, if you do not pardon and excuse the faults and offenses of others, you continue to punish others. You continue to harbor resentment, and that resentment will gnaw at you every time you remember that person, or any time someone does something that reminds you of that person. You will carry the painful memories in your resentment, and it will make you bitter inside.

We all know people who still blame their ex-wife or ex-husband for something. They keep talking about it and harping on it, long after anyone else is interested. This is not an attractive characteristic to have. Are you one of these people? Take a close look at your need to continue to punish others in your life.

Also, forgiveness is an ongoing process. Just when you thought you had truly forgiven a person, something will flare up in your memory, and it seems as if you are starting at square 1 again. This is especially true if the person has hurt you deeply. As you grow and heal, however, it is like a flower opening petal by petal. New layers of understanding unfold before you, and new opportunities to forgive arise. It is as though your consciousness gives you only as much as you are able to deal with at one time. When you become stronger and more healed, more of the pain is released because you are strong enough to handle it.

So stop holding grudges and forgive the people in your life. If you hold on to feelings of hurt and pain, you only punish yourself. Many medical theories connect emotional blocks with medical problems such as stress. You are the one who will benefit from forgiving.

The following exercises are designed to assist you in forgiving your past loves. Do them all, in the order presented.

Find yourself a quiet space and give yourself some time to do them. Make sure to breathe deeply as you do them. Breathe in and feel yourself filling with love and compassion. Breathe out and let go of the desire to punish. Breathe in again, bringing in love and understanding. Breathe out the need to punish. Keep this up for as long as possible. Just keep breathing in love and breathing out pain.

Open-Heart Forgiveness Technique

In a quiet place, breathe quietly in and out. Feel the breath coming in to the area of your body where you imagine your heart to be. Breathe into the heart, then breathe out of the heart. On each breath, imagine that there is a big, beautiful flower beginning to blossom where your heart is. Choose any flower that you love—a rose, a gardenia, a lotus. Imagine that gorgeous flower blossoming with love and forgiveness, with trust and compassion. Breathe in and out until the flower is completely opened, spreading its petals full and emitting the loveliest fragrance imaginable.

That is the smell of forgiveness and love. Breathe in the wonderful fragrance and let it fill you and heal you. Now send that flower to the person you are forgiving. Imagine it arriving in the mail or delivered by a florist. Imagine the happiness the other person feels as he or she realizes that this is the flower of your forgiveness. Δ

Punishment and Forgiveness

Make a list of all the people in your life whom you have trouble forgiving. Now, using a separate piece of paper, write one name at the top of it. Let yourself answer the following statement: "I want to punish you because . . ." and fill in as many answers as you can.

Once you have filled the page, turn it over and write, "When I think of you I want to punish myself because . . ." and write all the reasons you want to punish yourself. Once you have filled both sides of this paper, you will have a very good idea of the issues you are holding on to.

Now consider the possibility of forgiving the person. Wouldn't it be a relief to just let bygones be bygones? Let that person off the hook and stop being a victim or a martyr. Remove all punishment to yourself and to the other person. Declare yourself complete with that person or relationship, and move on with your life. The best is yet to come. Δ

Eileen was recovering from a devastating divorce. She had experienced the trauma of walking into her own bedroom to find her husband making love with a teenage girl from his office. She had a tremendous amount of anger and pain about the incident and toward her ex-husband.

She committed herself to a plan of self-healing, and she worked very hard in therapy and at home to release her anger and rage. She just didn't feel she could forgive her ex because the images and the pain were so vivid.

Finally, after two years, she experienced a release, and saw clearly that she was only punishing herself by holding on to the pain. Her ex-husband had long since remarried the younger woman, and was happily living his new life.

Eileen was the only person still suffering, and she finally decided that she deserved better. She knew that it was time to forgive him and get on with her life. She was tired of punishing herself.

The story has a happy ending. Eileen was able to attract her ideal life mate after about another year of intensive work on herself. It took three years for Eileen to heal herself, but it was well worth the effort.

The Theatre of Forgiveness

Imagine that you are walking into a very beautiful, old, ornate theatre. Over the door is a huge sign that reads "Theatre of Forgiveness." Appearing on the marquee are pictures of all the people in your life whom you need to forgive. Buy your ticket

with your willingness to let go of old hurts, and walk into the darkened auditorium.

Find a comfortable seat and let yourself see an ex-lover walk on stage. With total detachment, as though that person was simply an actor in a play, watch the individual as he or she acts out his or her life story. See all the hurt and fear that the person carries from childhood; see his or her heart's desire.

Now imagine that person receiving all the things that he or she wants in life. See the joy filling the person as he or she finally receives the rewards worked for so hard, the riches that have eluded the person, the glory that he or she longs for.

Shower all these riches on the person as you watch. Now see that if that person had what he or she needed, the individual could have given you much more of what you needed, too. But he or she couldn't. That person was just doing the best that he or she could at the time.

Applaud as the individual takes a bow, and let your ex-lover walk off the stage and take a seat in the audience.

Do this with the next ex-lover or spouse, and the next, until you have worked through your broken heart, healing and forgiving each inch of the way.

Now have yourself walk up on stage and see yourself receiving all the things you long for in your life. Watch yourself as you are showered with all the love and riches and beauty you have longed for.

And now become aware that the audience, filled with all the people you just forgave, is applauding and giving you a standing ovation. See that they all love you and want the very best for you. Take a bow and receive their love and applause as you wipe a tear of joy from your eye. Thank them and take another bow, and another, and another. Δ

◪ POWER TOOL 3

Releasing the Past

Forgiveness is the most powerful tool for healing the past, but some people have a difficult time forgiving. The next best tool is to simply *release* the past. You do not have to forgive to do this.

By releasing and letting go of the past, you will increase your personal feelings of love and aliveness. Remember, you are the only one suffering! You are the one who feels the pain, not your ex-lover. Chances are that your ex is long gone, off enjoying a new life and new loves. Your decision to release and let go of your past is your decision to release *yourself* from pain.

Do *not* dwell on the bad things. The more you wallow in the pain, the more grudges you hold against your ex-partner, the more stuck you will be.

The pain you feel will only end up harming you; your ex-spouse does not feel the pain. If you hold onto it, *you* get to feel it. How long do you need to suffer?

You can choose to let go of the pain *right this minute* if you like. It is your choice. You can choose to let it all go; bless, forgive, and move on.

Gaining Distance

First things first. Move out of the house you shared. If possible, move to a new part of town where you will not accidentally meet.

It may seem obvious to separate yourself physically from an old relationship, but it's amazing how many people do not do this. It is very important to actually move away from the old situation and to experience a new environment.

Give yourself a chance to heal and grow without the constant reminder of old problems and old situations. Move to a new apartment or house, or totally change the decor of your current house. Give yourself a sense of fresh new beginnings by changing your physical environment.

To gain distance mentally and emotionally means to separate yourself from the problem. One way is to see it from a distance, as though you were a huge giant watching the problem or incident on a small chess board down below you.

Be up above the situation and look down on it, gaining distance and awareness as you watch the problem as if you were watching a game on a playing field. By mentally separating yourself in this way, you can see the relationship or situation with a new perspective and understand it better. Δ

In his book Mastery, Tim Piering calls this technique the "meta-position" because you mentally assume a position above and apart from the problem "below" you.

In her book Feel the Fear and Do It Anyway, Dr. Susan Jeffers uses a similar technique. She suggests that you create a grid and write the names of all the functions in your life in the squares of the grid. When you fill in all the squares with words such as career, sports, family, and all parts of your life that are important to you, you begin to see that the box in the grid labeled Past hurtful relationships is really quite small. Once you put it into perspective with all the other parts of your life, the importance of this one area is minimized.

James was having a terrible time getting over his last relationship. After living together for three years, he and his lover had broken up abruptly when she expressed her desire to see other men.

He walked around New York City brokenhearted for several months. Every time he began to feel like he was getting over her, he would run into her on the street or in a restaurant, and he would become depressed again.

As it turns out, James was an actor and he was cast in a touring show at about this time. He left town for eight weeks and toured all over the Midwest, performing. He met several interesting women in the cast of the show, and began to enjoy being single again.

By the time the show had ended, he had put enough distance between himself and his past lover, physically and emotionally, that he felt great about life and about himself again.

What Didn't Work

Think about your past love relationships and begin to make a list of all the things you didn't like about your previous partners. Start by writing "It didn't work because he/she wasn't _____." Once you have made this list, take a long time to look at it and see that the relationship really wasn't right for *you* because of the reasons listed. Once you really grasp that it wasn't right for *you*, the releasing and forgiving process will be easier. Δ

Unmailed Letter

This is a letter that you will not send. It is a chance to vent all your anger, hurt, sadness, pain, and grief in the form of a letter.

You write this letter for yourself, as a tool to help you release past hurtful relationships.

Start by writing "Dear_____," exactly as though you were starting a letter. Now let yourself become angry and write about your anger. "You make me so angry because_____" and "I hate you when you_____," "I hate the way you_____" and write a paragraph or two about the ways this person makes you really angry.

In the next section of the letter, share the sadness you feel. Let the grief out in sentences that start "I am really sad about _____," "You really hurt me when you_____." Tell the ways that person hurt you; let yourself write a couple of paragraphs.

In the next section of the letter, let yourself express the sadness about the way you treated that *other person*: "I hate myself for_____" or "I am really sorry that I hurt you when I_____." Let yourself write a few paragraphs.

Now finish with a paragraph telling the person that you appreciate all he or she has given you, all you have learned, all the love you have received: "I do love and appreciate you and I will always remember the ways you_____" or "I know that we are both better off and I am thankful for_____." Then seal the letter in your journal or throw it away.

Do not mail the letter, because the person will not be able to understand the intensity of emotions you are sharing. It is a therapeutic tool for *your growth*; it is private and not to be shared with anybody.

Write an "unmailed letter" to all the people you hold a grudge against, everyone you are having a hard time releasing or forgiving. Δ

Joan was having a hard time releasing her ex-husband, even after two years of separation and divorce. She would think about him, remember the love they had shared, and recall the fun times they had together.

She got a call from him that really helped her break the spell he had cast over her. As they talked on the phone, he acted somewhat seductive and mentioned that he missed her. Furious, she hung up the phone and decided to try the unmailed letter technique.

She wrote and wrote, venting her rage and fury. She raked him over the coals for "missing her" when he could have had her heart and soul, forever. She wrote until she had fully expressed her pain, her sadness, and all of her feelings toward him.

She then placed the letter on a large rock in her backyard. She set the letter on fire and watched it burn, melting away all her resentment. She released him as the pages turned to ashes and blew away.

Re-Framing

Remember an incident from your past that was very painful. Close your eyes and imagine that incident again, like a movie running inside your mind. This time, make the movie black and white and speed it up like an old silent film. Now slow it down again and, as the movie plays, see a parade of colorful clowns frolicking in the background. The clowns laugh and make silly faces, wiggle their ears and hands at the characters in the movie, and do whatever else clowns usually do.

Find yourself laughing at the ridiculous antics of these clowns, and know that the incident is now changed in your memory. The memory is re-framed forever in your mind, and will never carry the harmful reaction it did before. Whenever you think of that painful incident, you will remember the clowns, and have to laugh about it. Δ

Bless and Thank Past Lovers

This is a rather advanced technique that uses the power of blessings as a releasing tool. In this process, you not only forgive and release the past but you also thank it for the learning opportunities it has provided.

Thank the person you loved and see how his or her behavior helped you to learn, grow, and evolve. This may seem like an impossible task if you are still holding on to the memories of pain, but it is a powerful healing technique. Once you can see the learning that this past relationship has offered, you can honestly thank your past partners for helping you learn.

You must heal the past, heal yourself, and take responsibility for creating those past experiences that helped you grow. Once you complete the old relationship, you are free to move ahead and experience levels of love you may not have believed possible.

Thank your ex-lover or spouse for all the gifts that he or she gave you during the course of your relationship. By blessing and thanking the person, you free yourself to move forward in your life.

You do this by sending the partner thanks telepathically. You do not need to contact him or her in person; this process is for your own healing and does not necessitate opening up old wounds. Send love and thanks, and lovingly place those old relationships in another place in your consciousness.

Think of these memories as gems in your treasure chest of life experiences, each a gift of love and learning. Choose to interpret your past this way, and you will make great strides in the healing process. The sooner you can do this, the sooner you can move on to attracting positive loving relationships. Δ

List the Good Things

List the good things that you received from a recent relationship. There are many gifts you received and things you learned. List them, no matter how small or silly they seem. Make a thorough and complete list of all the good things your ex-partner did for you or gave you. There are many more than you might think.

Even if the most positive thing you can think of is "exhaled carbon dioxide that gave the plants something to breathe." Start with that. You will find more and more things to appreciate as your list gets longer. Δ

◪   POWER TOOL 4

Develop a Positive Attitude

You can choose happiness right now. Believe it or not, it can be as simple as that. You have the ultimate choice in how you view life. Are you a half-empty cup or a half-full one? Are you optimistic? Or do you choose to see life as a constant struggle?

Why not choose to see the sunny side of life and love? The decision is completely yours, though for some people it is almost impossible. The simplest things are usually the hardest, if you think so. If you decided that it's easy for you, then it is. Choose the best that life has to offer, and decide that you deserve the best. Take a deep breath, and choose to be happy.

Don
. . . .

There was a point in my life when I felt that things were not working the way I wanted them to. I went to Bora Bora and spent a month on the beach, reading books, meditating, and looking inward to make changes.

One of the books I read was Joseph Murphy's *The Power of Your Subconscious Mind*. Though this book is full of excellent information, I got a lot out of one section in particular that dealt with the power of making conscious choices.

I began to realize that I had the power to choose everything in my life—the power to choose my actions and also the power to choose my attitude. I decided to choose happiness, and it has become one of the cornerstones of my personal inner work. I consciously choose happiness several times during the day, mostly first in the morning before I really wake up. Here is the exercise I use.

Morning Wake-Up

Each morning, as you wake up, say to yourself, "I choose happiness today. All things work for me today because I know deep in my heart that I am a good person and I deserve the best." By starting each day in this manner you are choosing to begin a life of sheer joy. **Δ**

Make it a habit to be positive and happy. Most people form a pattern of seeing the negative aspects of life when it is easier and much more powerful to choose to see the positive. Count your blessings several times a day. Take note of all the wonderful things in your life—your family and friends, your leisure activities, your skills and talents. Soon you will develop the habit of attracting good experiences and relationships to your life. The greatest things in life are simple and pure: the beauty of a spring flower, the full moon drifting in the summer sky, the smile you give a stranger.

If you choose unhappiness, that is certainly what you will experience. Some people wake up each morning convinced it will be another lousy day. Guess what kind of day they end up with? People with this attitude have to consciously retrain their minds. Whenever there is a negative thought creeping up, think of the exact opposite thing. If you feel yourself fearing it will be "another lousy day," radically shift that thought to the opposite: "today is going to be a fantastic, incredibly beautiful, and successful day."

Begin to explore your level of commitment to life and to appreciating and loving yourself. Take action to change destructive patterns, and know deep in your heart that you deserve love.

■ POWER TOOL 5

Use Your Sense of Humor

Try to see humor in your past relationships, and you will be a happier, healthier person. From a certain point of view, all relationships can be seen as hilarious. Seeing the humor in your own life will help you gain perspective on yourself and you'll also have a lot more fun.

People with a good sense of humor seem to handle the ups and downs of life pretty well. If you can laugh about life, and at your own silly antics, you will probably be a healthier and happier person.

It may seem like a stretch of the imagination while you are in the throes of emotional healing, but at some point it will be possible to view your past marriages and relationships as comedic.

Personal Sit-Com

Pretend that you are a professional writer for a television sit-com. Maybe you write for your favorite show. Pretend that the hero and heroine of the show are you and your ex. Recall one of your more ridiculous fights or break-ups, and write about it as though it were a funny scene for the television show.

Most comics get their best material from past relationships, and failed love affairs are the funniest of all. The problems of love and foibles of people are the source of most comedy in movies and television, as well as the best material for comedians on stage.

Humor is spiritual and healing. All the world religions share the concept of the cosmic joke, the enlightened clown, the trickster god. The Greek gods played practical jokes on each other all the time. Maui, the demi-god of Hawaiian legend, was constantly tricking the older gods and stealing their power. Native American Indian myths are full of the antics of the wily trickster Coyote.

Laugh! Enjoy yourself. Surround yourself with people who are loving, positive, and fun to be with. Go to comedy clubs, funny movies, and entertaining theatre productions; keep your sense of humor about the process you are going through. Remember, humor is healing! You are healing yourself and becoming the most whole and loving version of yourself. When you become whom you are seeking to attract, your ideal life mate will appear. Δ

◪   POWER TOOL 6

Be Centered in Your Spiritual Path

Keep yourself centered during the healing process. The best possible way to do this is to follow your spiritual path. It doesn't matter what form of spiritual practice you choose—it is up to you—but keep up your spiritual work. Commune with your version of God, Life Force, or Higher Power. Go to church, participate in charity activities, work on your personal growth, pray, meditate, do yoga, or sing gospel tunes. Connect with your Higher Self every day, even if it's just for a few minutes.

The spiritual path is a healing path. You cannot help but heal yourself by working on your spiritual growth. We believe that all paths lead to God, and that all of human life is ultimately a spiritual path. We are all evolving souls, and we are learning a lot during our journey along the physical plane.

This planet and our bodies are teachers—opportunities to learn and grow through daily lessons. We are tested at every turn, and we are given the opportunity to triumph. Not only is the spiritual path the ultimate way to learn and grow but it is also a great way to find your ideal life mate.

We found each other through our mutual love of Huna, the ancient Hawaiian philosophy of Aloha (love) and healing. (Huna, which means "secret," is the study of ancient Polynesian religious, psychological, and healing practices.) Neither of us was looking for a partner through spiritual study, and yet that is how we ultimately found each other.

Stories like this are fairly common, many people have met their life mates through a mutual interest in church activities, charity work, and spiritual disciplines of all kinds. It makes perfect sense, really. Where else would you earnestly look to find a spiritual partner?

Following your spiritual path has many rewards. It should not be done with the conscious thought of finding your perfect partner, but it is certainly within the realm of possibility that you will do so.

Spiritual practice is enlightening in itself; no other reward need be offered. However, to find one's partner is a gift and blessing that qualifies in magnitude as divine grace. A life-mate partnership truly is a gift from God. It is the most beautiful gift you can receive. We are filled with gratitude that we have been given this gift, and we intend to cherish and nurture it for the rest of our lives together.

■ POWER TOOL 7

Replace Fear with Love

Fear is the cause of pain and disease. Most of the things we fear exist only in our imagination. When you find that you are afraid of something, face the fear. Look at it with courage and say, "I now release this fear. I do not need it in my life anymore. I replace this fear with love, compassion, and understanding."

Replace fear with love. Fear lives in the dark shadows of loneliness. Reach out to others, work on yourself, let the light into your shadows. The light of love will melt the fear. Love is the essential life-generating force.

Sometimes it takes years to free yourself from the programming of your upbringing, and to heal the negative patterns you may carry about loving relationships.

This is not a quick-fix situation. We have both worked long and hard on our personal growth and emotional health in order to create the relationship we have always wanted. We let our clients know right away that their challenges may be such that it takes many years of devoted self-healing before the love of their life manifests itself.

The price is high, but it is worth it.

Appendix A is a list and description of the wonderful books and programs we have used to develop ourselves and our work. Though we have assembled as many great tools and techniques as possible in this one book, the work of "clearing the mirror" is so important and consuming that we recommend you make use of all the other terrific books and workshops you can find in your area.

2.

Whom Do You Bring To Your Ideal Partnership?

Who are you in a relationship? Who have you been in your past relationships? What are your ideas about a healthy relationship? Who are your role models? What do you bring to the party? In this chapter you have the opportunity to discover who you are in love relationships, and find out how to take responsibility for who you have been in your past relationships so you can change the behavior that didn't work.

When you get a strong idea of the ways that you added to the success of past relationships as well as their ends, you will have some powerful tools for attracting a much better relationship to your life—and keeping it. With courage and honesty, admit to yourself the ways that you participated in the demise of your past loves. Get a clear look at some of your own past mistakes. Forgive yourself and bless the situation as a growth opportunity, then vow to change the behavior that was harmful to those relationships. Bring the learning and growth from the past into your new partnership, and let your next relationship receive the rewards of past lessons.

That way, you can bring the best and highest version of you to the relationship. You can activate one of the most magnetic tools of them all.

◪   POWER TOOL 8

Become Whom You Wish to Attract

You are working now to clear the mirror so that you will be able to attract the best and most loving life mate for you. You will only attract someone who is at the same stage of development as you are. The metaphysical principle here is that you are who you attract. You and your life mate are opposite reflections of the same mirror. The clearer the mirror, the clearer the loving relationship.

While you are working on yourself to bring the best version of you to the relationship, your life mate is doing the same thing. As you increase your self-esteem and your feelings of self-worth, you will naturally draw people to you who have a high regard for you. If you treat yourself with love and self-respect, if you strive to be the best version of yourself, you will attract someone with the same high ideals.

We have one client who worked very hard on herself to be the best version of herself. She participated in various groups and programs, increasing her personal power and sense of self-worth. She followed the techniques we teach here, with one small problem. She neglected to clarify that her ideal life mate should be *single*, and so she attracted a terrific married man who otherwise mirrored her highest qualities. Her self-esteem had not allowed her to really feel that she deserved the best, so she sabotaged herself in this way.

Do not skip steps. Otherwise, you will be using a very powerful technology to attract all the wrong people.

Let's take a look now at who you have been in your past relationships, so you can better understand the person you would like to be in a relationship. Would you like to become more patient and understanding? If you are, your new mate will be too. Maybe you feel that you can be more compassionate and gentle, or more willing to stand up for yourself and ask for what you want and need in your life.

What You Have Brought in the Past

Close your eyes for a few moments and picture yourself in your most recent relationship, or even the past two or three. Who were you? Did you bring your highest and best self to that relationship? Did you offer love and support, openness and vulnerability, only to have it rejected? Or were you rejecting it yourself in some way?

This is the time to conduct a thorough and complete self-inventory. Ask yourself if you are a person whom *you* would like to be in a relationship with. What are your good qualities? What are you willing to bring to a life-mate relationship?

Make a list of all the good things that you brought with you to a relationship. What were you willing to give? What have you given in the past? Think of this as a résumé for a job—the job of creating a wonderful, loving relationship. What are you proud of about yourself when it comes to being an ideal life mate? Make this a good, long list that you can add to all the time.

We often pick people who can't give us the love we need in the ways we need it. We choose to limit ourselves in relationships because somehow deep inside we don't believe we deserve to be loved. So start by looking at the areas of your life that are not working, then begin to devise a plan to improve those areas. If you have a problem about money, for example, you might attract a life mate who mirrors the same issue, or has an even worse case of financial despair than you do. You could decide to clear up the problems together, but why not start the process of resolving those issues *now*? Δ

Very few of us have had healthy role models in our lives when it comes to loving relationships and marriage. If you are one of the few people who can honestly say that they grew up in a healthy, loving family, where Mom and Dad loved each other and loved you, count yourself among the chosen few.

The patterns you carry inside you are the ones you learned growing up. You have a very strong emotional bond to the same kind of relationship as your parents shared, because it is the only one that you know. We are the products of our emotional environment, and yet very few of us want to create the same kind of marriage our parents had.

This is part of what you bring to any new relationship—it is your emotional baggage. We strongly believe that you can break the old patterns and change the way you want to be in your future relationships. These next three exercises are a great way to get started.

Mother Roll

Who was your mother in love relationships? Recall your mother in her marriage to your father. What was she like? How did she act? Make a list of the positive and negative qualities your mother brought to that relationship. Δ

Father Roll

Do the same with your father. Make a list of the ways he acted in his marriage with your mother. How did he treat her? What did he like to say or do? This is how you learned about the way men treat women in relationships. This was your earliest programming.

If you don't like the way these two lists represent marriage and love relationships, be aware that these are the aspects of yourself you will have to work extra hard to change. Δ

Mom and Dad

Pretend that you are watching a television show like "Father Knows Best" or "The Brady Bunch," where everyone seems to be one big, happy family. Now gradually let your inner screen fill with images of your parents interacting with each other. Notice if there was love and affection in their interaction. Notice what they disagreed about, and what they created together as a couple. Let yourself watch in as detached a manner as possible, seeing how the drama unfolds.

Now open your eyes and make a list of the ways that your parents interacted positively. On the back of the page, list the ways they interacted negatively.

Read through the list to see if any of these positive or negative features have cropped up in your own relationships in the past. Now you know where they came from. Δ

Changes to Make

Make a list of the areas you want to improve in terms of what you bring to a relationship. Take a good look at the ways you may have helped to create the problems in your past relationships, and list the behaviors you now want to change.

In case you can't remember some of the mistakes you may have made, or don't realize that they *were* mistakes, we have assembled a list that we call the Seven Deadly Sins, along with their remedies, so that you don't have to repeat these mistakes ever again.

We share these seven deadly sins so that you can be aware of them before you attract your ideal life mate. These sins are so deadly and so potent that they can ruin the very best love relationship. Get familiar with them, root them out, and vow to leave them in the dust. They have not worked in any relationship in the past, and they will not work in the future. Now is the time to release these tendencies. Refer to the seven deadly sins as you make your list of changes and improvements. Δ

Do not judge yourself for this behavior. Look at it, learn from it, but do not use this as an opportunity to criticize yourself.

Instead, heal the past and move ahead. Go forward with your new love and your new life. Do *not* think that these exercises necessitate contacting your ex-lovers. You do not need to call and apologize again, or open up your heart for more pain.

These exercises are for you—to heal yourself, to learn from the past. Let your next relationship benefit from the past mistakes; don't try to live the past. Go forward with your new love and your new life.

SEVEN DEADLY SINS AND THEIR ANTIDOTES

1. Changing Him or Her

Many people enter into relationships with the expectation of changing their partner. They fall in love with the other person's "potential." They see the parts that they love and make an inner vow to change the parts that they don't like. This is the deadliest of all traps.

You must love and accept your partner just the way he or she is, realizing that he or she may never change at all. You are able to change yourself, but you will never be able to change another person. It just doesn't work that way. In the course of life and your relationship together, your partner may change. Just don't delude yourself into thinking that you are the one who made the change in him or her.

ANTIDOTE: *Total Acceptance.* We do not expect you to become a saint overnight. These antidotes ask you to really stretch to become your most loving self. But the truth is evident. You cannot change people; you must accept them the way they are. You can point out to them the things you might like to see changed, but you cannot expect them to change. They probably never will. If you can love and accept your partner the way he or she is, you will be able to ask the person to accept you the way you are.

2. Placing Blame

It is often tempting to blame your partner for everything that is not working in your life and in the relationship. It is a false perception to think that any *one* person is to blame. The responsibility in a partnership rests evenly on both partners.

You must always take full responsibility in your partnerships. No matter what happens, look for the ways that you created whatever incident or situation is creating the problems—and vow to change that behavior.

ANTIDOTE: *Communication and Full Responsibility*. Take personal responsibility and communicate with each other fully. Use opening statements such as, "I can see how my doing [or saying] such and such may have created the seed of the problem. If I work on myself in this area it would certainly help the situation . . ." etc.

It takes a lot of courage to admit that you are wrong or that you are responsible. Be courageous; admit that you are not perfect and that your own actions and thoughts may have started the whole issue. Your partner will be so impressed by your courage and honesty that most likely he or she will also take responsibility and you will be able to really communicate with each other and look at the root of the situation.

If *both* of you look for ways to take more responsibility, it opens the relationship up in amazing ways.

3. Being Jealous

There is no room in an ideal relationship for jealousy. This is a union based on love and total trust, spiritual connection and respect. It implies that each partner is honest and conducts him or herself with integrity and commitment.

Jealousy is fear of future loss. Do not even think about letting this destructive pattern into your life. Grant each other respect and tenderness, and honor the beauty of your commitment.

Jealousy is like a tapeworm feeding on the inner core of love, living in the squalid dimness of fear. If you bring problems or temptations into the light and share them with each other, you will have a chance to turn the situation around.

ANTIDOTE: *Trust*. Life mates have a spiritual, emotional, and physical connection that is rare, indeed. You can look a lifetime to find it; some people never find it. If you are lucky enough to have attracted a love of this magnitude, you are responsible for its care and well-being.

This is a gift more precious than any other. Be careful and gentle, be loving and trustworthy. Choose to be committed regardless of temptation and to honor your partner and your commitment. Communicate, then reconnect with your Higher Self, your life purpose together, and your love. If there is a serious problem with jealousy and trust, we suggest couple counseling.

4. Holding Grudges, Taking Revenge

If you are holding a grudge about something, know that you are the only one who is suffering from it. The other person doesn't know that you are angry or upset; only you know and you are the one who feels the pain. Grudges don't work. They create walls impeding intimacy and trust; they impair communication and block forward movement in a relationship. You must learn to forgive and release an issue, not cling to it.

Forgiveness means giving up the need to punish—yourself or another. To punish is very destructive; to continue to punish by holding a grudge over time is guaranteed to turn the best relationships sour.

ANTIDOTE: Let it go. If you have an argument or a disagreement, come to a resolution together and then forgive each other and forgive yourself.

This is not just a light-hearted suggestion; it is essential. Forgive, truly let go of the argument, release it, and move ahead. If you cling to the pain or anger of the disagreement, it will compound and intensify, growing like a cancer inside you.

The next time a challenge arises, all the stored anger and hurt that is held in the grudge will come pouring out, causing damage and hurt far beyond its original magnitude.

So be sensitive to each other, forgive, and let the sunshine of love fill the hurt spaces. Know that your partner loves you and means the very best for you and for the relationship. Release and forgive.

5. Being an Extremist or Workaholic

One example of extremism is obvious in many people's addiction to their careers. But this also applies to extreme spirituality, celibacy, partying, or even going to the beach. Whenever one aspect of your life outweighs all the others combined, this is an area to examine.

There is a difference between leading an active life in a career of your choosing and being a workaholic. Many people are addicted to their careers, especially those who have been single for a long time. Careers become the pivotal point in a life that is otherwise boring or lonely.

You are not your career. You are a full, rich human being with many aspects to your personality and many interests. If you make your career the most important part of your life, year after year, decade after decade, you will have lived a career, not a life. Our society is based on consumerism and we are encouraged at every turn to spend, buy, own, collect, and hoard. We think we need so many things, and this drives us to need more money, working like slaves while our lives pass us by in a rush of business. Why?

Workaholism is a trap that will consume an entire lifetime. It will eat up your time, it will erode your marriage, it will sabotage the very essence of life you are striving to achieve.

ANTIDOTE: *Balance.* Take stock of your life. See where it is unbalanced, and make the time for your relationship that it deserves.

Become aware of all the areas of your life besides work. Family, spiritual activities, hobbies, sports and fitness—all have equal merit in a life that is balanced. Check in with yourself and see how long it's been since you took a vacation, or did something for the sheer pleasure of it. Be flexible, be able to bend and stretch to include all the aspects of a healthy, balanced life.

6. Criticizing or Using Sarcasm

Compliments strengthen you. Criticism weakens you, your partner, your relationship, and your self-esteem. Criticism gradually undermines a relationship and, ultimately, the love you both cherished.

We have all seen couples bicker with each other, make sarcastic jokes, and undermine each other. It is an awful feeling to be in the presence of people who are hurting each other in little ways. Perhaps they have convinced themselves that this is harmless banter, that they are just kidding around. But all one need do is look at the expression on the face of the other persons in the room to know that this behavior is perceived (correctly) as destructive, indeed.

ANTIDOTE: *Compliments*. Respect each other; honor your privacy and each other's feelings.

It is tempting to be clever at the expense of someone else, and your partner is right there asking for it sometimes. We all say and do stupid things, but that doesn't mean we should be openly humiliated with little smites and verbal jabs. When couples resort to this banter, it is because there are much larger issues under the surface. Avoid the temptation of sarcasm or wittiness. It is unattractive and unpleasant. And it is a no-win situation for the giver, the receiver, and anyone else in the environment.

7. Making Judgments

We are not the judge and jury in our relationships. We do not sit on a throne and pass judgment on others.

The urge to judge is part of our "inner editor" and conscious mind. The mind is designed to judge and weigh and evaluate situations for our self-preservation. On a basic level, this is necessary to our physical survival.

But it is not healthy to apply these criticisms and judgments to others—especially your partner. It is not attractive to be a "know-it-all," to be set in your way, or to be close-minded. As the parable says, "Let he who is without sin hurl the first stone." We all have our problems and we are better suited to work on ourselves than to judge the progress of others.

ANTIDOTE: *Openness*. Do what works for you. Every person is unique and special—each human being is on his or her own path—so don't judge your mate's stage of development. Concentrate on your own path, follow your passion and vision, and hope that you won't be judged, either.

These seven deadly sins are capable of destroying the most beautiful and positive relationships in the world. Don't let it happen. Be aware of their power and learn to spot ways they have crept into your past relationships.

If you observe them slipping into your personality again, do whatever it takes to weed them out. Do not provide an environment for their growth or you will bring them with you to your new relationship. Get rid of them in the earliest stages so that they will be relatively harmless. The longer they are ignored, the worse they will become. It's like a beautiful garden that gradually becomes choked with weeds. Weed out the little sprouts before they spread through the beautiful garden of your love.

THE POWER OF LOVE—SELF-FORGIVENESS

Most people carry enormous guilt around in their bodies and in their minds. It is very easy to judge and criticize yourself for past behavior.

Self-torture can take many forms: dredging up all the ways

you were manipulative and uncaring in the past, being extremely hard on yourself for the ways you treat your current lover, blaming yourself for all the unsuccessful relationships you have had, viewing yourself as too gullible and naive.

In order to experience the levels of loving connection that await, you must work to relieve yourself of all these demons from the past. Ask yourself if you are willing to stop "beating yourself up" for this past behavior.

Are you willing to stop punishing yourself? It doesn't help anyone and it only hurts you. So let all the hurts, remorse, and guilt fly out of your heart and out of your mind.

Don't blame yourself for previous mistakes. If you choose to allow yourself to love and forgive, start with this idea: "No matter what I have done in my life, I did the best I could at the time with the tools that I had."

It is cruel to sort through your life with the knowledge and hindsight that you possess now. Do not judge and blame yourself for previous actions and behaviors. You did not have the gift of foresight back then! You did not know and understand the things you take for granted now.

It is hard to realize this. We think that we have always had the insight and wisdom of the present moment, but it isn't true. You have been evolving. You have learned and progressed every day of your life. You have a wealth of skills and knowledge now that you did not possess last year. Imagine who you must have been ten years ago. Of course you were the same person, but you lacked the understanding you have now. If you had understood the things *then* that you do *now*, you wouldn't have behaved in the ways you did!

Love yourself enough right now to admit this fact. The following statement is an excellent mantra and our gift to you:

I did the best I could with the tools I had at the time. If I had known then what I do now, I would have done things differently.

You did not make a mistake! You did everything right. Perhaps you don't care for the methods you used, or the choices you made. You simply acted out of the limited awareness you had at the time. You can choose to change that behavior in the present and in the future. You can choose to forgive yourself *now* for the activities of your past.

Self-forgiveness takes a warrior's strength. It is easy to beat yourself up, but it is extremely *hard* to forgive yourself. Self-love will free you from the chains of the past. You can choose to wallow in the quicksand of self-hate and abuse, or you can choose to forgive yourself.

Grant yourself a pardon, give yourself a break. You have already punished yourself enough.

Self-Forgiveness

The chances are very good that the universe forgives you, we forgive you, all the people in your life forgive you, God forgives you, anyone you can think of forgives you.

Think for a moment of someone who you really love. Send the person love and forgiveness and see how that feels. Now take that same love and forgiveness and give it to yourself. Don't skimp at all here; give yourself a full measure of the same love that you regularly bestow on others.

No one else can forgive or absolve you; it is up to you. Δ

Now that you have forgiven yourself for who you were and what you did in the past, take the time to bask in the glory of who you are right now and who you will grow to be in the future.

This is a special time in your life. Being single is very special; it is a great time to really get to know yourself, to understand what motivates you, to discover your life purpose, and to change the things in yourself that are stopping you from having what you want in life. There is no doubt that you will attract your ideal life mate in the near future, once you have worked on yourself and you feel ready.

The following "Private Time" technique can be used to tune into the moment and appreciate this special time in your life.

Being Single—Private Time

Close your eyes and take a few deep breaths. Relax and envision a time in the future when you and your ideal life mate have found each other. You are in love and living a life of quality and joy together. Feel how it will feel, imagine how your life will be—the places you will go, the things you will create together. Really enjoy the scenario.

Now come back to the present and become aware of all the things that you can enjoy right now. You have the luxury of having the time to work on yourself and heal. Enjoy the privacy of being single for a while. This is a very special time in your life. Maximize its potential by really enjoying its unique gifts.

You can tune into the present by sending yourself into either the past or the future, exploring those other time frames and coming back into the present with renewed appreciation. This travel technique really makes you appreciate everything good about the present situation. We recommend using it often. It takes only a few seconds, like a quick daydream, and the results are very powerful. Δ

Things I Love

What do you love to do? What gives you pleasure? How long has it been since you gave yourself permission to have and do the things you love? Stop being so hard on yourself and give yourself the things in life that you love. Just for fun, make a list of all the things you love to do. You can break this into categories such as physical, mental, emotional, spiritual, or simply free flow and make a general list.

After you have the list, go back over it and write beside each item how long it has been since you experienced that activity. Suppose you wrote down "Dancing" or "Traveling." Then write next to it, "Went dancing last year on New Year's Eve" or "Went traveling just last month to Chicago."

This list will let you know what it is you really enjoy doing, and how long it's been since you gave yourself that pleasure. It can be pretty revealing to notice that you are sacrificing your life doing things that you do not enjoy. Δ

The good news is that it's not too late to put the things you love back into your life. Start now to really let yourself enjoy this lifetime. Life goes by so quickly. You turn around and ten years have passed. Make every year count, make every minute a pleasure.

Can you see yourself having complete pleasure and enjoyment in your life? Take a moment to reflect on this question. Let your imagination wander and see what it comes up with.

Take the risk. Make pleasure and enjoyment a primary goal in your life. You deserve the best; now let yourself have it!

Your Best Self

Who are you at your highest and best?—when you are operating at your top levels of love and joy, compassion and receptivity?

Close your eyes and take a few deep breaths. Relax into your chair and remember a time when you really felt good. Begin to form a picture of yourself at your very best. Think of a time in your life when you felt happy and strong, loving and loved. Get a mental picture of that person: this is you at your best, the you that is longing to get out all the time. This is the you that your ideal life mate is looking for—right this minute, somewhere across time and space.

How does it feel when your life is really working?

Now stand up and make sure there is some room around you for this next part of the exercise. Let the mental picture of your best self form again and begin to see this beautiful, strong, loving self forming right in front of you. See yourself at your very best, standing right in front of you, facing the same direction you are.

Get a good, clear, colorful picture and let yourself fill with happiness at the realization of who you really can be. Now let the emotion and love build up a little, and then take a step forward, right into the image of you at your best *self.*

Step into your true self and feel a shimmer of delight as that self merges with you and you become it. Let the strength and power fill you with joy as you realize that you have so much to offer, so much to give.

Now that you have the feelings of your best self integrated deeply inside, take a moment to write in your journal or on a piece of paper, "What are the qualities that this person brings to a relationship?"

Make a complete list of the wonderful qualities and gifts you bring to a partnership when you are at your best. This is the new you, the you that you intend to share with your ideal life mate. This is the you that person deserves to fall in love with, this is the *you* that you deserve to be. Δ

Once you accept the fact that life is a pleasure—that you can be living in heaven on earth, and that you deserve the very best—magic begins to happen. You begin the magical process by being open to it, by allowing the possibility of total joy to enter your life.

If you are blocked, or carrying around subconscious desires for failure and self-sabotage, you will limit the joyful potential of your life. You must believe that you deserve a life of happiness and abundance, and demand it of yourself. Don't settle for a mediocre life, for painful relationships, or for unfulfilling careers. Time is running out! Maximize your potential in this lifetime. Why wait?

What Qualities Would You Like to Bring?

What is a dream life? Who is your ideal lover? How will you spend your energy and your time on this magical planet together? The earth is the Garden of Eden if you just let yourself see and enjoy it. This is the pleasure planet, a place where dreams really do come true. If you have the energy and the desire, if you believe that all things are possible and that anything can happen, it will.

What are the special qualities that you would like to be able to bring to your next partnership? Make a list of some of the items that you know are important and worth developing in yourself so that you can give them as a gift to your next relationship.

Here are a few suggestions:

1. A healthy, beautiful, sensual body.

2. A great positive attitude.

3. Love, trust, and compassion.

4. Comfort and ease with myself.

5. To be my best self.

6. Commitment and loyalty.

7. Spiritual connection with my Higher Self. Δ

Use the techniques shared in this chapter to become more aware of what you are willing to bring to your next relationship. The things you are willing to give are the same things that you will receive, because your ideal life mate will be a reflection of all the best qualities in you.

3.

Opening to Wholeness

Because we attract people to our lives who mirror our own stage of evolution, it is important for us to first *become whole*.

In Chapter One you concentrated on healing past love relationships. In Chapter Two you took a hard look at who you have been in your past relationships and who you are now willing to bring to a new love relationship. In this chapter we share some of the finest tools we know for creating yourself as a whole and complete, loving and giving human being. This is the person whom your ideal life mate will recognize.

Use these powerful concepts and exercises to become the most loving and lovable you. Once you are a whole and complete person—ready to receive and give love wholeheartedly—you will be ready for your ideal life mate.

All love comes from within. It is not out there somewhere. A partner is not going to redeem you and magically transform you into a better, more loving, and more lovable person. That is up to you.

The adventure you embark upon is an internal journey into the most inner places of your heart and soul. You must connect with the loving and lovable parts of you. Once you discover these parts, you must enhance them and fertilize them so that they grow in the sunshine of trust and self-acceptance.

The joy of self-love has a ripple effect. When you are happy and enjoying yourself, this feeling rubs off onto the people around you, which ripples further from their lives, affecting their families and friends in a never-ending circle of joy. This circle of joy, rippling out into the world, is what will attract your life mate to you. Everyone loves to be near happy, whole people—and your ideal partner is no exception. Wholeness and happiness draw people to you like bees to honey.

If you feel that you are unworthy, that you do not deserve to be fully loved and appreciated, the tools in this chapter will help to build self-esteem, and your receptivity will increase. Many have forgotten how to receive. It is tangled up in issues of self-worth. We receive and we give; this is the natural cycle. Break this cycle at any point and it throws off the natural balance.

Openness, receptivity, and the ability to receive love are distinguishing characteristics of a whole human being. Once your heart is healed, it opens to love. So open up to receive what the universe has to offer.

Many religious and philosophical systems of the world maintain that the heart is the center of loving feelings and experiences in the body. Our Western culture links the symbol of the heart with love in everything from romantic songs to Valentine's Day cards.

The ability to give love and receive love in return is the domain of the heart. When you experience feelings of love you can literally feel your heart swell. Work on your ability to open your heart; it is the doorway through which your ideal life mate will enter.

Are you ready for your ideal life mate? Have you paid your "dues"? Are you willing to receive and give the kind of love you have dreamed of? Do you deserve the best?

To receive love you must first feel that you deserve love.

When you feel you are a loving and lovable person, you know that you deserve love. It is your God-given right. It is part of being a human living on planet earth. You don't even need to question it.

The path of self-discovery is very exciting. You are a complex and fascinating creature, and learning about yourself is a wondrous adventure. Here are some techniques, ideas, and exercises to learn more about the person you are and how to become more open, alive, and receptive to love.

◪ TOOL FOR BECOMING WHOLE 1

Compliment Yourself Often

This is not egocentric, as our Western culture might have you believe. Compliments and acknowledgments are like water to a thirsty plant. They build and repair shattered emotions, they create healing and wholeness. When you focus on the good, you empower all that is positive about life.

When you compliment yourself, feel the strength build within, feel your face break into a smile. A good technique is to compliment yourself for five minutes each day. Set a timer, and begin to acknowledge the good things about *you*. Make a list if it helps you to focus, but keep it up for the full five minutes if you can.

Also compliment others as often as possible. When you send loving energy to another, you benefit as well. Acknowledge people; thank them for doing a good job or for affecting your life in a positive way. Watch how they flower, how they smile; see how good it makes you feel.

Complimenting others has the same power as complimenting yourself. Criticizing others has the opposite effect, however. When you criticize others, you suffer as well.

Complimenting builds strength and confidence, is pleasurable and powerful, and makes you feel great to be alive. It is an excellent technique for building self-esteem and the inner knowledge that you deserve the best life has to offer. Affirm the positive. Acknowledge what is working in your life, and the gifts will increase.

Georgia, a 42-year-old woman, had never been married. She had been through a string of relationships but she wondered if she was just too independent and strong-willed to ever find a mate.

She began to switch her attention from self-criticism to compliments. She worked with the idea that there was someone just perfect for her—an ideal life mate who would appreciate her strengths and forgive her weaknesses. She complimented herself often, and focused on her positive qualities.

Recently she married her ideal life mate, a man who finds her strong independent streak charming. He is not threatened by her strength; in fact, he loves it. The quirky qualities that others might have criticized, he thinks are "cute." By complimenting herself, Georgia was able to re-frame her previous self-image, and attract a man who was perfect for her.

◪   TOOL FOR BECOMING WHOLE 2

Get Support

Support groups and various types of networking organizations have emerged all over the country for people going through all kinds of life transitions. There are support groups for the twelve-step programs such as Adult Children of Alcoholics, Alcoholics Anonymous, and Overeaters Anonymous. There are groups for people going through divorce and other relationships transitions. All of these are helpful as a person changes and grows. As you work on yourself and change, you may long to communicate your new discoveries with people who will understand you.

Mary

I was one of the original members of The Inside Edge, a dynamic group in Southern California that was created in 1985 to support people in the healing and human potential fields. I had never been a "joiner," but this group was unique. It was so supportive that I found myself becoming a cheerleader for the group. Every week there were fantastic speakers—authors and professionals on the leading edge of consciousness, healing, global change, and the human potential movement.

The speakers were incredibly inspiring, and the group itself consisted of about five hundred wonderful people. The members were very successful professionals in all fields. They shared a strong personal commitment to self-growth, peace, and improving the quality of life on the planet.

This support group added to my life and personal growth in many ways. I met most of my closest friends there. I took the workshops offered by the speakers and bought their books. As an emcee onstage every week, I grew in confidence and my ability to speak to groups blossomed. The benefits were enormous, and I am forever grateful to founders Diana and Paul Von Welanetz for creating an excellent environment for healing and learning.

Don

I attended Serge Kahili King's Huna meetings every Wednesday night on Kauai. The people who attended the meetings had taken Serge's workshops and had some understanding of Huna.

The support of the group, the healing energy shared, and Serge's brilliant commentaries were very inspiring to me and very helpful in my personal growth.

*   *   *

We are not saying that you must join a group of some sort if you want to attract your ideal life mate. But we are pointing out the importance of support and friendship. A sense of community and shared interests can be a very helpful support as you go through transitions in your life. You are working on yourself, you are changing, you are becoming the best version of yourself.

■ TOOL FOR BECOMING WHOLE 3

Follow Your Passion

One of the very best forms of self-understanding and therapy is to immerse yourself in work that you are passionate about. What do you *love* to do? What really gets you out of bed in the morning? What would you be doing with your life if you didn't have to work for a living? Where is your joy? Where is your passion?

Paul was a man in a fourteen-year marriage who recognized that the love, passion, and romance had long gone from his relationship. He would see romantic couples walking hand in hand, and it hurt him to realize that the romance and passion was gone from his life.

After working with his wife in therapy, they both realized that their relationship had become one of friendship rather than romance. Paul knew that he wanted and deserved a partner who was as passionate and willing to share romance as he was. He had the courage to change his life, work on rebuilding himself, and soon he attracted the love of his dreams.

Most people deny themselves the things in life that they really love. Life is short! Now is the time to follow your passions. Ideally, you will be able to find meaningful work in the area of your passion, but if not, at least give yourself the time to follow your passions as a hobby.

If you love to sail, maybe you can find work that is on or near boats. If not, maybe you can find work on a magazine devoted to sailing and ocean life. At the very least, you can find a way to go sailing on weekends.

Ken and Patty met while on a skiing weekend in Aspen, Colorado, last winter. They are both ardent ski buffs and they spend as much time as possible on the slopes. The mutual love of skiing was what brought them together and, one year later, they are still in the midst of a wonderful romance.

Follow your passions and you will meet other people who share those passions. Follow your passions and you may meet your ideal life mate.

What Do You Want in Your Life?

Take a moment to reflect on what your life might be like if you really deserved the best and were able to attract it to you. "The Best" means whatever is the best for you. Some people might consider immense wealth to be "The Best"; for others, a small beach cottage on the rocky coast of Oregon far away from civilization might be "The Best."

What is the best for you? Think about this, then make a list or write it in your journal. Explore the areas of your life and decide what would be the best for you in your career, in your family life, in your physical or mental health, and your emotional well-being.

How much money do you want? What type of life-style? What appeals to you? What would you like to be doing with your days? Who would be sharing this dream life with you? Would you travel around the world or spend more time alone? Define some of the parameters of your dream life. Δ

DREAM GOAL BOOK

Here is a technique that Mary has been using for years. It allows you to understand what you really want in all areas of your life.

Rather than carrying around vague ideas of what happiness is for you, once you create your Dream Goal Book you will have tangible evidence that you are creating a dream life. Once you know that you deserve the best, you can achieve it and track the results of your achievements.

This is not kid stuff; it is a very powerful technique for impressing your subconscious mind. As you may be aware, there are different areas of your brain that respond to different stimuli. The left side of the brain is the logical, scientific part; the right side responds to feelings, creativity, beauty, and intuitive or emotional input.

The Dream Goal Book is designed to engage both sides of the brain. The goals you write down and the results that you enter will activate the left side of the brain. The pictures and poetry will appeal to the right side. The goal book has a powerful effect on your brain and therefore your whole life, if you let it work for you.

Just as with the other techniques shared in this book, use the goal book as a tool only if it feels good. Otherwise, move on to tools and techniques that excite you, because those are the ones that will work the best.

Keep your goal book going until you have completed the goals you set for yourself, or make a goal book for each new year. Start the year by defining the areas you want to work on and setting goals. Add new goals during the year whenever you want. Make the book fun and make it effective for you.

Tracking your successes is a powerful way to build self-esteem. As you achieve your goals you will begin to realize that you are a very powerful and effective person, and you really *do* deserve the best that life has to offer.

Start by purchasing a three-ring looseleaf notebook large enough to hold several hundred pages. Buy lots of lined three-hole paper and some colored construction paper for fun. You will need at least five dividers with label tabs to separate the book into the areas of your life. Collect lots of magazines, stickers, travel brochures, and the like.

You are going to create sections of the book by making a distinction between the different areas of your life where you want to create powerful results. Write the following words on the labels and dividers:

Love Life

This is the section where you create your ideal life mate. You can cut out pictures that give the right feeling, and write down the qualities you would like your ideal life mate to have.

This is also where you write what you are willing to *bring* to the relationship, as well as any other ideas, poetry, or goals that pertain to this space of your life.

Career and Money

Collect pictures of your career goals, financial goals, and all the other things you would like in your life with your future prosperity. Make lists of written goals that you would like to achieve in your career and your finances.

Personal or Spiritual Growth

This category is for your personal growth and development. It can reflect whatever you want in your personal life—the vacations you would like to take, the peace of mind you seek, the books you want to read, the plays and theatre you want to see. Include pictures, ticket stubs, programs, dried autumn leaves— whatever excites your imagination and makes you want to make these dreams come true.

Mental Improvement

Perhaps there are classes you wish to take, languages you want to learn. Maybe you want to listen to personal growth tapes, take seminars and workshops, learn the computer, study for a new career. Anything that pertains to mental development goes into this section of your goal book.

Physical Beauty or Image

Do you want to lose weight? Join a gym? Take yoga classes? Get a new hairdo? It is a lot of fun to cut out all the fashion, accessories, and beauty supplies your heart desires and paste them into this section of the book. As you cut out pictures in the top fashion magazines, you will begin to see an emerging "new" image for yourself. Let yourself go in this section of the goal book!

In each of these sections, you will be writing your goals in each area of your life. To illustrate these goals, you can create a "treasure map" by collecting colorful pictures from magazines of the things you want to create in your life. You can really have fun being artistic as you create collages filled with the images of things that you want in the various sections of the book.

You will be recording the results of your projects and keeping track of your progress in general. Feel free to make more sections if you so desire. These five are very important, but add extra sections if there are other areas of your life you want to work on.

You may want to create special sections for special-growth projects. Let's say that you want to heal an area of yourself such as your relationship with your father. You might make a section titled simply "Father," and set up a program for improvement. You might decide to see a therapist for six months to work on the issue; maybe you decide to read five books about father-daughter and father-son dynamics; and you vow to write him ten letters and cards in the next three months that express your love and appreciation. Make a page for each of those goals and write them down.

As you achieve each stage of success, write down the accomplishment and date it. When you have completed the entire project, write "Hooray" and "Congratulations," and paste stars and hearts all over the page. Celebrate yourself for completing the project and acknowledge the steps you've made in reaching your goals.

It is really thrilling at the end of the year to look through your Dream Goal Book and see all the goals you crossed off and the projects you completed—all the dreams that you made come true.

Sensory-Based Mini-Vacation

To become sensory based is such a pleasure, and such a relief from the constant overload of the conscious mind that it is like taking a mini-vacation. It only takes a moment and it brings profound happiness and joy.

Tune into the present moment—what is really happening right now, this very instant. That is the only thing that is real; the rest is imagination.

If you tune into the moment, you might hear birds singing, or sounds of the wind. You might be able to smell and see things—the way the light plays upon the pages of this book, the colors and shapes around you. One of the most pleasurable ways to tune in to the present is to become sensory based. That means simply to become aware of the senses and the messages they are sending your brain.

Bring your attention into the present as many times as possible during the day. Become aware of the way things look and sound. Tune in to any smells or tastes near you. Feel the touch of the objects in your environment. Feel the softness of your own skin; touch your hair and feel the texture. Place your hands on the back of your neck and gently massage for a few seconds—feel the instant pleasure and relief this brings. Listen to the sounds around you and close your eyes to hear the sound of your own breathing, your own heartbeat.

Open your eyes and notice something in the environment that is green, something that is blue, something red. Feel the temperature of the room—is it warm and cozy or cool and soothing? Take a deep breath and let out any tension you are holding in your body. Stretch your face and your body. Smile to yourself at the incredible improvement in the way you feel after just a few moments. That is becoming sensory based. Welcome back from your mini-vacation. Δ

One of our clients was a busy career woman who was so stressed out, so nervous, that she found that she was smoking all the time. She felt constant tension in her body, yet she longed for an ideal life mate. We pointed out to her that, at this point in her life, she would simply attract someone as stressed out as she was. We began to try various techniques to help her relax, and to ground her in the present.

We saw that she was never in the present—she was always living in the past or worrying about the future. We tried the sensory-based mini-vacation with her, and it really had an impact. We could see her begin to relax as she let go of her concerns about the future and focused her attention on enjoying the present.

Time and Space Travel

Here is another technique we discovered to bring your attention to the enjoyment of the present. We were traveling for an extended period of time, and it was the first time that Mary had been on such a long vacation. At about the two-week mark, she began to experience slight anxiety about being away from working on the book for such a long time. She felt anxious to get back to Hawaii and back to writing and the beach. These feelings of homesickness could have jeopardized a wonderful vacation, but Don came up with an excellent process to help Mary bring herself into an appreciation of the present. Here is what he said:

> Close your eyes and let yourself drift back to Kauai. We're back in the beach house now. You are getting up every morning and writing the book. You are back in your special routine and it feels great. We are taking beach walks and lying in the sun, brainstorming and writing, working out, making love, going to the movies and out to dinner. Good. . . .
>
> Now we have been back for a week. The routine is wonderful and we love it. And now we have been back for two weeks. We're getting a lot done on the book; the beach is wonderful. Life is beautiful. And now we have been back for about three weeks. And you find yourself thinking, "Wouldn't it be nice to take a little trip somewhere?"
>
> Now come back into the present, here we are in the middle of a wonderful vacation, and we have two weeks left! What would you really like to see and do? What can we do

here that we won't be able to do back at the beach house? How about some museums, culture, and a few concerts in the park? Isn't it fabulous that we have enough time to really enjoy ourselves here before we head back to the beach? Let's make the most of it!

This traveling technique was really effective. Whenever Mary felt herself losing her center, she took a quick "trip" back home, then came back into the present moment refreshed and ready to keep traveling. Δ

Inner Gifts

∽

Don used a wonderful daily technique last Christmas that he called the Twelve Gifts of Christmas. Each morning he would lie in bed, still half asleep, and ponder the gifts he wanted to give himself that day. One day it might be the gift of inner peace and happiness, another day perhaps the gift of health and harmony. Upon rising, he would write the gifts of the day in a Christmas card to himself and place it under the Christmas tree. The Christmas season was especially abundant for him because he felt the tremendous gifts become part of his life each day.

We have modified this gift technique to be usable year-round. Here is a list of gifts to give yourself for each day of the week. Write this list on a card or piece of paper and put it by your bedside. Look at the list each morning and let yourself drift and meditate on the implications of that gift in your life. Let yourself gradually wake up to the beauty and power of each gift each day.

Sunday—Inner peace and happiness

Monday—Confidence

Tuesday—Love and abundance

Wednesday—Success and prosperity

Thursday—Trust and joy

Friday—Appreciation and gratitude

Saturday—Health and harmony

Give yourself these gifts and compliment yourself often. Really acknowledge what a terrific person you have turned out to be. Make lists of all the good qualities you have and thank yourself. It is very important to appreciate and acknowledge yourself. Celebrate your successes and victories, and create celebrations to emphasize your accomplishments. Δ

▨ TOOL FOR BECOMING WHOLE 4

Make Enjoyment a Goal

What if the purpose of life was pleasure? What if each incarnation on earth was simply a joy ride, an exploration of the human body and emotions designed as a curriculum in ecstasy? What would that mean in terms of addiction to suffering, pain, and fear? What would you have to give up to experience life as a gift of bliss?

Enjoyment is the purpose and the goal of human life—just enjoyment, that's all. You are not required to do, or be, anything other than who you are. Your job this lifetime is to enjoy this beautiful planet and this beautiful human body.

An understanding of this deceptively simple concept could change your world completely. Enjoyment and appreciation can give you different priorities in your life, enhancing and improving it beyond belief.

There are so many advantages to enjoyment that it just may be the secret key to happiness and saving the planet. When you enjoy, it gives the people around you a chance to be happy. You positively affect and change others through your own enjoyment. Simply by enjoying a situation you can improve the experiences of others.

Sara was a single woman who lived in New York City. She worked very long hours at a demanding job. We realized upon meeting her that she wasn't having much fun in her life, and we introduced the concept of enjoyment as her new goal in life.

Together we created a program for her whereby she had to view every single thing in her life from the point of view of enjoyment. She was to rate all the parts of her life in terms of enjoyment. If the enjoyment level was too low, she had to stop doing that thing.

Using this criterion, Sara was able to look at her life in an entirely new way. She began to question how hard she was working and for what rewards.

The concept of enjoyment as a goal changed Sara's entire life. She has fundamentally changed the way she dresses (the old way wasn't enough fun), the way she eats, the places she goes, the friends she makes, the trips she takes, and so on.

▨ TOOL FOR BECOMING WHOLE 5

Share Happiness

Make it part of your life to spread happiness and enjoyment to all you meet. Begin to consciously choose to enhance the quality of people's lives around you. As a result you will find that your life improves dramatically. It is fun to give to others, and it is extremely rewarding. Give the gift of your love, your thoughtfulness, or your attention.

Awaken the part of you that loves to do fun things, and let yourself enjoy spontaneous activities. As grown-ups we restrict our movements and our creative expression. Reconnect with the happy child inside of you. This child never really grew up; it still lives in you and it wants to come out and play.

The inner child will reward you with many gifts if you let it out once in awhile—the gift of spontaneity, of happiness and laughter, the gifts of innocence and trust. Let the little girl or boy in you come out and play.

"Love Yourself" is a phrase we hear all the time in the consciousness and healing professions. But do we really stop and think about what it means? Loving yourself means knowing you are the most perfect and beautiful version of you that ever was or ever will be. There is only one you, and there will never be another. You are absolutely the finest manifestation of *you* available at this time. Appreciate that fact, and give thanks. Acknowledge yourself, accept yourself, love yourself.

If you can't love yourself, how do you suppose someone else will be able to? They can only love you to the extent that you love yourself.

To heal and love yourself is to *be* the beautiful, compassionate, loving being that you are looking for in the outside world. When you are able to be the ideal life mate for you, the ideal love partner will find you.

4.

Embracing the New Male and Female

Things are really changing about the ways that women relate to men, men interact with women, women interact with women, and men interact with men. It is time to bring mutual understanding and compassion into our relationships—to listen to the suffering of the other sex as together we heal our wounds. Men and women who have hardened themselves, who have become numb for the sake of their role in society, are cracking open the armor, healing old dysfunctional behavior, and reaching out to each other.

Here are some of the exciting things we are noticing about women and men, and the new ways they are relating to each other: more gentleness and true compassion, increased respect for each other, the end of manipulation, and a willingness to connect deeply, spiritually, and emotionally with each other.

Of course, there are profound differences between men and women too. Biological differences, for one, can really shed a light on the past challenges men and women have had to face in relating to each other. But these challenges also present an opportunity for each sex to become more compassionate and understanding in an attempt to communicate with each other.

We are not the same. We are not designed to be the same, and therein lie the excitement and adventure.

If you have strong opinions about the things men are "supposed to do" and the things women are "supposed to do," it's time to change those ideas and limitations. We live in a unique and challenging time. Men and women both work outside the home, both cook and care for the children, and both maintain a household and lead busy, full lives.

If you find that you have some imbedded concepts about what the sex roles "should be," weed them out right now. They will undermine all your efforts to find an ideal life mate and all that you attempt to create in your partnership together.

Think about the ways you would like to share responsibility in your life-mate relationship. Think about this in terms of finances, household chores, travel plans, child care, entertaining, and every other area of life.

Cherish the sexual differences between you, but don't lean on outmoded definitions of sex roles. It is time to break from all the old stereotypes. Maybe he loves to cook and clean up; maybe she loves to mow the lawn. Maybe she makes more money and is the one who understands investments and finances. Maybe you hire a maid to do the heavy house cleaning so neither partner will be bothered.

Be flexible and open. Allow the strengths of both partners to enhance a union, and don't limit your future relationship with arbitrary rules.

Be open and willing to communicate about the shared responsibilities of your relationship. Be careful not to assume gender preference. Opt for equal rights and equal responsibilities.

We believe that there are male and female aspects of every human being, and that our goal is to balance these parts into one whole being. Understanding your own inner male and female helps us to understand and better relate to people of the same and opposite sex. When these two forces are in balance, the whole and complete human being can find a mirror that is also whole, complete, and balanced.

In our workshops we separate the men and women for about one hour. Don takes the men and Mary takes the women for a personal, in-depth discussion of what we call "Men's and Women's Magic." We are pleased to report that at least one-third of our workshop participants are men. This is a sign that a growing number of men are admitting they are ready to find an ideal lover and partner.

THE NEW MALE

There is a growing "men's movement" that has been called the new tidal wave of consciousness. It is picking up where the women's movement of the seventies left off. Men are gathering together to explore male initiation, masculine psychology, and being a man in this society. They are discussing their feelings about everything, including reverse sexism or "male bashing."

The challenges for men are greater than ever before. They must be strong providers and athletic sportsmen as well as sensitive lovers, gentle friends, and supportive fathers. They feel the pressure to be both masculine and feminine, active and passive.

For the past few decades, it has not been easy to be a man. In the same respect, it has not been easy to be a woman. It's time to heal cultural and familial wounds.

Men are finding the emotional support of groups of other men that women have depended upon for the past ten years or so. Many authors and workshop leaders are addressing the needs of men who want to be both sensitive and open, while maintaining a strong sense of their masculinity. They ask the question, "What does it mean to be a man?"

Men are analyzing the realities of growing up male in this society. In the process they are discovering the social conditioning that all little boys receive, and the incredible difficulties they face in breaking away from this conditioning.

Sam, one of the men in a recent intensive-workshop weekend, longed for a life-mate relationship. He was attractive, intelligent, and had a quirky sense of humor that many women would find appealing. The only problem was, they never got a chance to speak to him to find that out.

We discovered that Sam had a double-whammy stopping him from relating to women. First, he had very high expectations; his ideal life mate is very beautiful and in perfect physical shape, she must be exotic and intelligent. Second, Sam was so painfully shy that if he should somehow attract this goddess, he wouldn't have the courage to talk to her.

Using the techniques in this book, we helped Sam get a clear picture of his ideal life mate that wasn't so heavily influenced by the physical. We also had him concentrate on the exercises in chapters two and three, to develop his self-esteem and increase his confidence. Since the physical seemed so important to him, we got him enrolled at the local gym and put him on a body-building program to get him more connected with his own body.

Sam is doing just great. He has started to feel better about himself and, therefore, is less judgmental of others. He is meeting women in great shape at the gym, but he is also a lot more compassionate with those women whom he attracts who may not be specimens of physical perfection.

Sam, along with many other men, has been conditioned by the social structure of growing up male in America. He has been fed images of perfect women via magazines and the media. He thought those pictures were what a perfect woman must look and act like, until he faced the cruelty of those impossible ideals. He also discovered that once he stopped expecting women to look like television actresses, he felt a lot more confident and comfortable around them. He broke away from the conditioning that makes women into fantasy creatures rather than living, breathing human beings.

Poet Robert Bly has been leading men's workshops at the Ojai Foundation in California for over a decade. He uses myths and archetypes of warriors, hunters, kings, and poets to help men get in touch with their essential masculine archetypes.

Men have a pantheon of inner archetypes to draw from. There are many ways to be a man, and ideally a man has access to the wide variety of personalities that live in balance inside him. He can draw upon the king, warrior, magician, lover, father, son, wild man, builder, hunter, farmer, and so on. By contacting these archetypes men are able to get in touch with their loving, joyful, passionate, masculine strength.

The Inner Male

On a clean piece of paper, create a column down the far left side. In the column, make a list of the following inner-male arche-types, leaving plenty of room between each one: king, warrior, magician, lover, father, son, wild man, builder, hunter, wise man, farmer, priest, teacher, and any others that come to mind.

Meditate on each word, gaze at the word, and let any images, feelings, sounds, or thoughts appear in your mind. After each word, put a check mark if you feel a place inside you resound to that concept. Write down any thoughts, feelings, or memories that this word may have generated.

Some of the words may leave you cold; just pass them by and move on to the next word. If a word strikes an inner note, let your imagination go and allow the images evoked by the word to fill you. Write those images down while you remain in a meditative state.

After you have worked through the list, analyze the words that resonated for you. Also pay careful attention to the words that left you completely cold. This list is the beginning of a map of your inner sense of masculinity. Δ

Men's Magic

In our culture, there has not been a safe space for men to reveal some of their deepest issues. During the Men's Magic section of our workshop, the men have the opportunity to do some intimate relating with each other. They are very open to hearing what the other men have to say about their experiences in relationships.

Don usually opens up the discussion by asking the men for ideas, advice, and techniques that have been effective in creating intimacy, sensuality, and connection in their past relationships. Often there is a period of shifting, nervous laughter, and jokes until the men settle into a real open discussion. Humor tends to break the ice as the men start to share with each other.

Bill is a perfect example of the things that come up for the men in this section of the workshop. Bill is a good-looking, successful contractor. He is the kind of man to whom most women would be very attracted, yet his girlfriend was leaving him. He came to the workshop to discover what he was doing "wrong" in his relationships.

During the Men's Magic discussion, Bill became very embarrassed when the conversation began to turn toward sex. He laughed and blurted out, "You mean it's not enough to watch the news together in bed and then roll over on top of her?" Everyone laughed, but the statement revealed a deep fear of intimacy, the very thing that was causing his girlfriend to reject him.

Bill was amazed as the other men began to share the ways they created intimacy with their lovers. They mentioned talking, touching, and caressing; back rubs and massages; holding each other and cuddling for hours; holding hands; and spending quality time that was not oriented toward having sex. These ideas had never occurred to Bill. He had thought they were unmasculine, but as he listened to the other men, he realized that he was the only one in the group *not* doing these things. He had a revelation about what men can do to share intimacy with their lovers, and he expanded his definition of what it means to be masculine.

The men really appreciate this section of the workshop. Many say afterwards that it was the most beneficial of all the exercises and techniques shared. In some cases, it may have been the first time in their lives they have been in a sharing environment with other men. They usually feel a breakthrough just from the actual experience of being together—much more than what was actually said or the words that were used. Being together is what is valuable.

What do men really want from women? Compassion, openness, gentleness and understanding, sensuality and fun, romance and excitement—these are the answers that we hear to that question in our groups.

What are the concerns of men? How to be a good husband and lover, father and friend; how to provide for their family; and how to find enough time to enjoy each other. Single men are concerned about AIDS, and are not interested in promiscuous sex. They are really ready to find a life mate and build a life together.

Men are tired of feeling the brunt of the world's ills. They are tired of being blamed for everything from making war to destroying the rain forests. They are tired of being bashed as responsible for 2,000 years of patriarchal society. They are sick of being blamed for relationships that haven't worked out. They seek an end to the guilt, and they appreciate compassion and love, forgiveness and acknowledgment.

How are men healing themselves? They are reaching out to

the women in their lives. They are opening up to male friendships and bonding experiences. They are attending twelve-step groups in ever-growing numbers and taking workshops. They are seeking therapy. They are looking at themselves differently, and they are demanding to receive the compassion and respect that they are willing to give others.

THE NEW FEMALE

What does it mean to be a woman today? This is a topic that comes up frequently, mostly in relation to women's interest in goddess archetypes, Jungian psychology, and their own inner search for the feminine.

Using the pantheon of goddess archetypes, women are enjoying new ways to know themselves as women. There are hundreds of major goddesses; every culture in the world has wonderful goddess imagery and artwork to study. The most prominent goddesses that women relate to, however, tend to be the Greek and Egyptian or Mediterranean goddesses. These archetypes represent aspects of women as lover (fertility), mother (nurturing), daughter (virgin), warrior (hunter), balance (judge), death (recreation), creation (birth), as well as many others.

The goddesses allow women to see that they are much more complex and many layered than they had thought, possessing aspects of all of these major and minor arcana of femininity. It is exciting to look into yourself and discover the ways that you are like other women, and that you embody the essential qualities of womanhood. It is freeing to observe that you are not just one way or another, but that you have many aspects and therefore many points of view.

The women's spiritual movement is fulfilling something very deep for many women. It is in many cases the first authentic experience they have had of spirit, or nature, or life force. The following exercise will bring you in touch with your inner archetypes.

The Inner Female

On a clean piece of paper, create a column down the far left side. In the column, make a list of the following inner female archetypes, leaving plenty of room between each one: queen, warrior, sorceress, lover, mother, daughter, wild woman, teacher, crone, dancer, priestess, and any others that come to mind.

Meditate on each word, gaze at the word, and let any images, feelings, sounds, or thoughts appear in your mind. After each word, put a check mark if you feel a place inside you resound to that concept. Write down any thoughts, feelings, or memories that this word may have generated.

Some of the words may leave you cold; just pass them by and move on to the next word. If a word strikes an inner note, let your imagination go and allow the images evoked by the word to fill you. Write those images down while you remain in a meditative state.

After you have worked through the list, analyze the words that resonated for you. Also pay careful attention to the words that left you completely cold. This list is the beginning of a map of your inner sense of femininity. Δ

Women's Magic

Without fail, in the workshops, when Don takes the men out of the room, the women's first response is "I wonder what they're saying" or "I wish I could be a fly on the wall to hear the guys talk."

Why do women care so much what men are saying? Because they want to understand men better? Or is it because they want to gather information and ammunition to use when they are with them?

Many women feel so cut off from men that they really don't have a clue what men are like—what they talk about and think about. Women want more information to try to understand men so that they can relate to them better, and also so they can try to better influence the men in their lives.

The problem for women is that they *cannot* make men feel the way women want them to—not really. That has got to come from within. Oh, a woman can work on communicating more effectively with a man; she can use all the latest psychology to analyze him. Ultimately, he feels the way he does, or doesn't. If she tries to manipulate him in the areas that really matter, such as deep loving or commitment, she will suffer in the long run.

One of the things we talk about during Women's Magic is the similarities and differences among fantasy men, movie stars, and the guy on the street.

The major movie stars of our time are men like Harrison Ford, Sam Shepard, Tom Selleck, and Kevin Costner. Stars like these are adored by women from all walks of life. How have these guys become today's dream men? Is it by playing the part in a movie of a highly paid stockbroker? How about a surgeon? A dentist?

Turns out these heartthrobs have roles as baseball players, inept private eyes, military guys, drifters, space ship repairmen, and so on—blue-collar jobs for basic, heterosexual males. In the movies these characters have down-to-earth jobs yet the men have tremendous inner strength, poetry, gentleness, and appeal.

Put these same guys on the street of a big city and they wouldn't get the time of day from those career women who drool over them on the big screen. What is going on here?

As women have become more and more successful, the

margin of space for a man to be more successful, more highly paid, more educated, and more talented in comparison has shrunk. How many men fit the description of the single gal's perfect man? He has to be sexy and poetic, as well as highly paid and successful. He has to be tuned in to her feelings, and also dangerously, ruggedly handsome.

Does this fantasy serve anyone? Maybe it's time we put it to rest.

In the movie *Dances with Wolves*, Kevin Costner plays a military man on a remote outpost. He is not highly paid or successful. As the movie progresses, he grows tremendously as a human being. He is a beautiful, compassionate, poetic soul. Women all over the country have fallen in love with this image, with the character, and with the actor playing the character in the movie.

Yet if we change the time from the Old West to the present day, how many women would lose sleep over a lone military guy on a remote outpost? Sure he's attractive and poetic, but every modern single woman would wonder if she could be happy with a serviceman's salary out in the middle of nowhere.

Several years ago Tom Selleck, in "Magnum P.I.," was the ultimate symbol of male perfection for many women. Yet when you analyze his character on that television show, he was really just an overgrown boy living with a rich friend with questionable personal income. His room was a mess and he could hardly organize his life. He drove a borrowed car and solved murders. What self-respecting woman would long for those qualities in a man?

What is so appealing about a man like this? Is it that he is fundamentally unavailable? He is, after all, a made-up character, not real flesh and blood. What can we learn about ourselves from our attachment to these movie stars?

Which would you prefer: a man who makes a lot of money as a top surgeon but is never home or has a beeper with him in bed? Or how about a poetic carpenter who builds houses by day and sings to you at night? What is the best for you? Something's got to give, and it is media programming. You deserve more than a two-dimensional celluloid screen version of a perfect man.

Go beyond the trap of the superficial package. Look for depth and heart, not a made-up character. You deserve more! Have high expectations. You deserve the best, but focus on the inner qualities rather than the packaging. Look for the inner qualities and the outer manifestation of them.

One of the cruelest tricks in our society is the way men are made into "success objects."

We would like to put an end to the concept of "marrying down." We have to release such outdated concepts.

Instead, how about a new archetype? Team work. Visualize yourselves helping each other up the mountain of life—like mountain climbers, you and your ideal life mate. One goes ahead and then throws down the rope for the other, and you balance and protect each other on the steep climb. Working as a team in life is a more powerful image. Neither of you is marrying up or down, over or under. Both of you are equals, part of the team.

Stanley and Iris is a lovely movie starring Jane Fonda and Robert DeNiro. Stanley, played by DeNiro, is fired from job after job, and Iris, played by Fonda, discovers it is because he can't read. Stanley finally lands a job as a bathroom janitor, yet he is a man who designs, invents, and builds huge contraptions in his garage as a hobby.

Iris slowly teaches Stanley to read. Despite many setbacks, he has the courage to confront his fears and he learns. He eventually gets a good job in Detroit and comes back for Iris, freeing her from a life of virtual poverty. That is team effort.

Iris could have decided Stanley was just a janitor and not worth her time, but she believed in his ability and she taught him to read. He had the courage to evolve; she had the courage to see below the surface.

If we women all had the courage to see below the surface, we would find *there are plenty of terrific men out there.* There has been a lot of fear and talk about how there are "no men out there anymore." This is something single women talk about constantly, in groups, at restaurants, on the phone, to their therapists.

There are plenty of *men who don't hate women at all.* Women have become increasingly aware of their desire to change men. The books in the eighties that dealt with the issue of "men who hate women" brought up a lot of good points to explore. Women must take responsibility for choosing the men in their lives. Women must also have compassion, must know that every human being is on his or her own life journey, learning the lessons that he or she needs to learn.

The truth is, there are lots of terrific men out there. But they may not fit your previous definition of what you think you need in a man. There are men of all cultures and races, all over the world. There are younger men and older men. There are working-class men with much potential for love and growth. But there are not very many surgeons and stockbrokers who love the arts and can listen to you talk about your feelings as they fly you away to the Bahamas for the weekend.

It's time to wake up. Time to get a little more realistic about what you want, who you are looking for, and where you can find him. It's time to break free of society's programming.

When you know that you deserve love, you will have it. When you are willing and able to give love, support, and partnership, and you know with every part of your being that you deserve the same kind of love that you are giving, you will find it.

Remember, you are the mirror of what you will attract. Start by *being* your ideal man or woman, and your ideal life mate will come along.

Part Two

ATTRACTING

LOVE

◢

Now that you have worked to heal yourself of past loves and have got a sense of yourself as a whole, complete person, it is time to take action—magic action.

The techniques shared in this second part are designed to create major changes in your physical world—to create something where there was nothing, to take a dream and manifest a perfect partner. They are powerful physical and mental techniques that use emotional energy to work with the laws of attraction, such as visualizations, affirmations, treatments and prayers, journaling, celebrations, rituals, and guided imagery in deep trance. The metaphysical laws or energy dynamics they encompass are shared by most every religion or philosophy as well as by most systems for creating success and excellence in human lives. They work because they convince your subconscious or subjective mind of the importance of your desire for a partner. Once all parts of your subconscious mind are activated and aligned, it can work wonders to attract your ideal life mate into your life.

Our beliefs about who we are and what we can do affect what we are able to accomplish. Most religions base their philosophy on the power of faith, belief, and prayer. If we believe in magic, we'll live a magical life. If we believe that our ideal life mate is somewhere across time and space looking for us, he or she is. Whatever you believe is possible, is true. Belief is the fuel that propels your mind.

Whether you believe you can do something, or whether you believe you can't, you're right. Beliefs are like commanders to the brain. They give the brain a framework within which to create. Belief delivers a direct command to your nervous system. This is why a placebo works. If people believe a pill will heal them, it will, even if the pill is only sugar.

Your beliefs are your choice.

In this part you will learn the powerful steps to attracting and manifesting change in your life. You will be using these tools to attract your ideal life mate: the power of faith and belief, a focused mind, effective action, emotional fuel such as energy and passion, and a developed receptivity and acceptance.

In Part One we asked you to use *all* the exercises to heal your past loves and clear your mirror. In Part Two, feel free to use whichever techniques and exercises appeal to you. (The only exception to this is Chapter Five's Five Qualities of Satisfaction list—that is a *must*.) Mary has had incredible success using celebrations, rituals, and power objects in her healing and manifestation work. Don prefers visualization techniques and deep inner work to achieve powerful results. It is a personal choice.

So as you read and learn about various techniques, be aware of those that seem to resonate in your inner being. Once you discover the exercises that work best for you, use them every day or as often as possible.

So, let's get started. It's time to attract your ideal life mate.

■

5.

The Five Qualities
of Satisfaction

The Five Qualities of Satisfaction form the guidebook and road map you will use to identify your ideal life mate.

To recognize your ideal life mate, you must know who he or she is. You will attract many people in your life, especially once you start to practice these techniques. So you must be very clear about who it is you are looking for, so that you will recognize your partner once he or she arrives.

Most people have a very muddy picture of the person they want as their life mate. This is one reason why they haven't successfully attracted a partner. The clearer you are about your requirements for your love partner, the better chance you have of attracting the right person.

By doing the exercises in this chapter, by making the extensive lists and probing your own beliefs about the characteristics of your ideal life mate, you will discover exactly who he or she is.

One of the most important decisions in life is choosing a loving partner and a romantic relationship, yet men and women alike make unwise decisions when it comes to love. We carefully choose our college or other training, our careers or jobs, yet when it comes to love we rely on "fate" and "chemistry" and other fleeting emotional reactions to determine this extremely important aspect of our lives.

Why do we leave this important choice to random emotional impulses? Because we "react" rather than "choose" our lovers and partners. We throw all caution to the wind and leap into an emotional whirlwind, hoping that everything will work out because it "feels right."

Often, what "feels right" in the beginning turns out to be part of an unbroken pattern from our past, and we find ourselves in another relationship with all the troubles of the last one.

Instead, give this choice the same significance and importance you would any other life-changing decision. By knowing exactly who you want, and acknowledging that you deserve a quality love relationship, you open yourself up to receive a new kind of love. By declaring that you are ready, you have already taken one of the biggest steps and have started the magic.

The Thorough and Extensive List

Begin by making a list of all the qualities you would like to have in your ideal life mate. There is no way to cut corners here; write down *everything* you can think of. Be very specific.

Remember a time when you felt totally loved. What is absolutely necessary for you in order to feel totally loved?

Here is a sample of some of the things you might include:

Likes to have fun

Wants to have a family

Enjoys music, theatre, culture

Committed to a spiritual path

Dresses beautifully, has a sense of fashion

Works out, stays in shape

Is a vegetarian

Loves the way I look, compliments me often

Keep going until you have at least *fifty to one hundred* qualities written down. Now add the qualities you know would really make a relationship work. Qualities such as:

Willingness to be emotional and vulnerable

Shares household responsibilities

Supports my career goals

Great sex (explain what that means to you)

Aligns with my life goals

Healthy in body and spirit

No addictions

Now let yourself just cut loose and put in a few qualities that you can't imagine anyone being wonderful enough to fulfill. Examples might be:

Surprises me with dream vacations and weekends

Extremely romantic, lots of flowers, cards, and gifts

Adores me

Listens to me

Thinks she or he is the luckiest woman or man on earth to have me Δ

What You Didn't Get

Now start a second list that includes all the things you wanted in your past relationship(s) but were unable to get from your partner. These will be very clear in your mind, simply because you wanted them before and there will be emotional energy stored there.

You want to make sure you get these qualities in the next relationship, so write down everything you can think of. Δ

What You Are Willing to Bring

This is a list of all the qualities you are willing to bring to your life-mate relationship. Maybe your listed qualities will be something like being willing to let go of the seven deadly sins once and for all. These can be something you are willing to let go of, or willing to bring. Δ

The qualities you have listed in these exercises are very important. They are the keys to creating an ideal life-mate relationship. So take your time and complete all of these exercises.

The qualities that you come up with ultimately are not arbitrary. They are deeply thought out and culled from experience.

The Five Major Qualities

Using the lists you have just made, begin to look for the five major qualities—five major points that you really *must* have in order to be truly happy in a relationship. There are *five* major points that you must discover.

Go over your first three lists with a fine-tooth comb and pick the five qualities that really are important to you. Many times these will incorporate several other points on the list. Look at all three lists to see if there are qualities that reappear several times. Chances are, these are qualities that you really want your life mate to have.

Find the five that you really can't live without in a life-mate relationship, then write your five criteria on a separate sheet of paper and memorize them. Δ

This process is very illuminating because you will learn, once and for all, what is really important to you in a mate. It may not be easy; you will have to work to figure out which five points are the most important, but it is well worth the effort. This exercise will help you to focus much better. The clearer you are about what you want, the better your chances are of creating the best relationship for you and attracting the right person for you.

If you carry hundreds of criteria around in your head you may forget the most important ones. But if you have a strong, clear picture of the five major qualities, you will be able to run a quick checklist and discover whether someone in your life has them or not.

Why five? There are many magical things linked with the number five: cubits in the Bible were five feet long, there are five sides to a pentacle or pentagram, five points to a star. Five represents the central number in numerology. It opens the door leading from individual to partnership and community. The message of the number five is curiosity, new thinking, and expanding change. It is an ideal number for adventure, growth, good fortune, and new opportunities.

But the most practical reason is that five is easy to remember. This may seem simplistic, but remember what it is like when you first meet and fall in love or lust with someone? You are in a whirlwind of emotions and hormones; you certainly aren't thinking straight. These five qualities are there to ground you, to help you get your bearings in the midst of an emotional and sensual cyclone.

If you are with a person who seems that he or she may have the qualities you are looking for in a life mate, run quickly through your Five Qualities of Satisfaction, counting them secretly on each finger, and get an immediate idea if this person is a possible partner. This will give you some stability just when you need it most.

Sticking to your five magic qualities can be a difficult process, however. Sally, a women in her early thirties, had to make a difficult decision after she discovered her five magic qualities.

When Sally first discovered the five qualities for her satisfaction, she was dating a man who was very supportive. But in creating her list she discovered that he met only two of the five criteria. Three major qualities were missing in him. She gave this a lot of thought, then told him that she wanted to see other people.

Painful as it may seem, she felt it was better to break off with this man in order to keep the path clear for her ideal life mate to come into her life. She decided she would never know unless she tried, and she vowed to wait for a man who had all five qualities she wanted. She met her ideal life mate within two days of making this decision, and one year later they were married.

We can't overemphasize the importance of this exercise. You

must discover the Five Qualities of Satisfaction, otherwise you will be pulling in lots of people who are not right for you. The universe will provide what you are looking for once you make a clear request. Once you know what you are looking for, you will be able to recognize the qualities in the people you meet, and gauge whether they have one, three, or (hallelujah!) all five qualities.

Ideal-Life-Mate Qualities

Here's a suggestion for setting up the ideal-life-mate section of your Dream Goal Book. Take five separate pages and write one of your Five Qualities of Satisfaction at the top of each page. Cut out pictures that remind you of that quality and paste them into the book on that page, or collect snapshots, or poetry, or phrases that seem to evoke that quality and glue or write them in.

Make a smaller section within the life-mate section that evokes the physical representation of your ideal life mate. How tall is he or she? What physical qualities does he or she have—grace and elegance, physical health and athletic ability? Have fun as you cut out pictures of faces, smiles, eyes, and so on and put them in this section. Romantic images are very good to include—pictures of lovers and wedding couples, hearts and flowers, whatever you feel like. Δ

There is no way to avoid doing this work if you are serious about attracting your perfect life mate. Do not skip lightly over this section and expect the rituals and techniques in the following chapters to be effective. Take the time to really tune in and discover what your personal criteria are. Get clear about them, write them down on a piece of paper that you keep in your wallet, memorize them. They are very important and very magical.

Now that you have discovered your magic qualities of satisfaction and have done a few exercises with those five, we share the qualities Mary came up with.

We purposely left this until the end, because we wanted you to come up with your own qualities rather than using ours. Of course, if you like the ones we have included, you are free to exchange a few for yours. Just make sure that the five you select are really the five you must have in a relationship.

MARY'S FIVE QUALITIES OF SATISFACTION

1. *Great sense of humor, playful and fun.* "I never realized how important a sense of humor is to me until I dated a man who had *none.* I come from a family of funny people, who love to tell jokes and entertain each other with stories and a witty turn of phrase. All of my friends are writers or otherwise creative people, mostly in the entertainment industry, and they are extremely funny people. This quality is extremely important to me."

2. *Terrific sex.* "This is self-explanatory, but it needs to be personalized. Terrific sex for me may not be terrific sex for you. I know what my brand is; be very specific about yours."

3. *Doesn't need to be trained.* "This means he has practiced a spiritual path, had enough therapy, experienced human potential seminars and growth workshops. In other words, he has worked on himself, just as I have."

4. *As smart or smarter than I.* "An active, alive mind is very important to me. I like smart people, curious, growth-oriented risk-takers who are passionate about learning and who love to use their minds creatively. I wanted a life mate who was able to keep up with me and also teach me a lot."

5. *Has achieved a level of success in the world financially where he is generous with himself and generous with me.* "One way our society acknowledges success is by financially rewarding the efforts. I wanted a man who had proved his value and worth to society and to *himself,* so that he had a feeling of confidence and self-esteem. It was important for me to allow myself to receive some financial support from someone who was generous and had fun with his abundance."

Those are Mary's five criteria. Feel free to use any of them that you wish, but give yourself the choice to change and improve on them. This is your list, your criteria. Make it work for you and your life mate.

We know a couple who used a list of qualities in an unusual way. George and Jennie had known each other socially for about a year. They were friends and they used to flirt a little bit now and then, but they had never gone out together or dated.

One day they were joking about finding their ideal life mate, and Jennie mentioned that she had her list in her purse. George asked to see it, and Jennie suddenly felt very shy about showing it to him.

He persisted and finally she let him see the list. As he read it over, his face began to shine. He looked at her and said, "This list sounds like me."

"I know," she replied. "That's why I was afraid to show it to you. I don't want to destroy a great friendship."

"But I'm the guy," he persisted. "I'm everything you want in a man. It says so right here. Let's go out for dinner; I want to see what happens." He smiled.

They went out and their friendship turned into romance. They had a whirlwind courtship across Europe and they are now happily married.

This is a true story. We know it sounds too good to be true, but instead remember it is "good enough to be true."

6.

Action for Attraction

This chapter is about taking new and effective *action* to attract your ideal life mate. So far, we have done a lot of inner work to prepare for attracting your new partner. Now it's time to take some action with the outer part of ourselves—our bodies, our life-styles, and the way we operate in the world.

Before taking any action, always know your outcome, or exactly what you want. Then you can take actions that will produce the results you desire. Get feedback, and see if what you are doing is working to attain your goals. If not, be flexible enough to change your approach.

You've already established part of your desired outcome by developing your Five Qualities of Satisfaction. Now it's time to get a clear picture of your desired outcome in terms of your own life.

Desired Outcome Exercise

Take three pieces of paper and write a short paragraph or two about your desired outcome on each page. Be specific. Be positive. At the top of the first page write "How will I feel?" and begin to describe your life with your ideal life mate and how you feel about it. Write about how happy and fulfilled you are.

On a second sheet of paper write "How will I act?" Visualize yourself in the relationship and imagine the ways that you will be acting, moving, and behaving in your new role. Write about it.

Do the same for "How will I look?" on the third sheet of paper. Describe the way your hair looks, the way your face looks. Now describe your body. Does your body look different from how it does right now? How does it look different? Δ

Now that you have established your desired outcome, let's look at some ways to take action and get the results you want.

◪   POWER TOOL 9

Become an Attract-ive Person

If you want to attract someone (your life mate) or something (love), it follows that you need to *become* more attract-ive. By attractive, we do not mean you need to look like a movie star or a *Vogue* model.

Become a more attractive *you*. Working with your mind, body, and spirit, become the most attractive version of yourself that you can. Be attractive mentally, physically, and emotionally.

The first three chapters of this book were dedicated to clearing your mirror and increasing your self-esteem so that you can create more healthy and successful loving relationships. The emphasis was on becoming mentally and emotionally attractive.

Now it is time to look at the physical aspects—your physical body, your image, and the ways you use your sexual energy. Making physical changes in your actions, your environment and location, and the roles that you play in your life can all contribute to a new attract-ive you.

YOUR BODY

Your body reflects the way your feel about yourself. It represents the outward manifestation of your inner state of awareness. Your body is a mirror of who you are, your self-esteem, and your self-love.

How does your body respond to feeling and pleasure? Honor what works for you. Avoid activities that are harmful or self-destructive. They can be a form of self-punishment, a reflection of the deep inner conviction that you're not lovable or deserving of love and happiness.

As you work on yourself to improve your self-esteem, you will notice the changes that take place automatically in your body. The body responds beautifully to love and attention. It is a gorgeous container for the beautiful being that inhabits the temple. Take care of your body; take care of yourself. You deserve to be healthy and happy, satisfied and filled with pleasure.

The body craves exercise. If you deny this craving, your body will punish you with aches and pains, irritability, and even illness. It takes a lot of energy to manifest change in our lives. Your body can provide that necessary energy.

A strong, healthy body sends a message of pleasure and vitality, builds self-esteem, and rewards you with looking and feeling terrific. Get into shape; be the best *physical you* that you can be.

You do not have to be a Madison Avenue version of physical beauty, but be the best you. Find several forms of exercise that you enjoy and begin to treat your body to them on a regular basis. Your body will assist in your emotional healing process by lending sheer physical strength and vitality.

A beautiful, strong, healthy body is one of the most loving and beautiful gifts of being human. Our bodies are designed for pleasure, for sensual joy and vitality. Be good to your body; give it good food and exercise, and give it healthy sexual experiences.

Your body is your devoted slave. It does whatever you request of it. Try being good and kind to your body, and thank it for all the good things it provides.

YOUR IMAGE

Your image is the sense of style and personality that you project in the way you act, dress, speak, and carry yourself. Your image is one of the major ways you send messages out to other people. To attract your ideal life mate, be aware of the image you project. This many seem simplistic but it is amazing how many people overlook things like image and posture when analyzing themselves. These are visual messages about your inner self that you offer to the universe.

Take a look at your closet and analyze your sense of personal style. If someone were meeting you for the first time, what kind of information would he or she gather about you from your clothes? Do you always dress in the latest fashion, or do you haunt thrift shops to find vintage antique clothing?

What messages is your choice of accessories sending to the world? Do you always wear a thick leather biker's bracelet? How about a dainty crystal around your ankle?

How about your posture? Do you stand up straight with your head held high, or do you slump over and walk as though you hope no one can see you. Your posture sends out many messages about how you feel about yourself.

Many women tend to take the layered look in fashion to an extreme. Are you so layered that no one can see you in there?

It is an easy way to hide, but it will not help you attract your ideal life mate. Men love women's bodies, and they love to have the chance to see and appreciate them. This doesn't mean you have to dress inappropriately, but it does mean that there are tasteful ways to let your personal style reflect your beautiful body.

And for the men, the same thing applies. Don't hide under baggy clothes and unstylish fashions. Take an interest in your image, improve it, and you will attract people who you never even thought would look at you.

That's the great thing about fashion. It is totally democratic. Anyone can be in fashion simply by updating one's wardrobe. You only have to spend a few dollars and suddenly you are fashionable.

So spend some time developing the image that reflects who you are today. Ask your best friend to help you with this project; it's always good to have an objective opinion. There are specialists in most major department stores and also professional image consultants you can contact if you feel you need help.

SEXUAL ATTRACTION

Nature is on your side. Since the laws of nature are oriented toward growth, reproduction, and survival of every species on earth, Mother Nature is moving enormous energy to help you find your ideal life mate and ideal lover.

Birds do it. . . . Bees do it. . . . Mother Nature wants you to do it also. We human beings are blessed with an enormous amount of sexual energy and attraction for each other. Sexual energy is the most immense power there is. We all have this power; the question is, how will you use it?

This abundant and glorious sexual energy can be used to attract your ideal life mate. Focus this energy and you will increase your chances of success. How do you do this?

1. Don't diffuse it. Don't weaken this energy by scattering it all over everybody all the time. Hold your sexual energy close; it is a beautiful gift.

2. Channel the energy toward meeting your goal of attracting your ideal life mate. Direct it toward attracting the right kind of people, the ones who might fulfill your Five Qualities of Satisfaction.

3. Honor it. If you let this energy spill all over the place and attract the wrong partners, you will make the task harder in the long run.

The body is the pleasure center. It is incredible just how generous and extravagant the gift of physical pleasure really is. Your body is a beautiful temple of love. And honoring that temple means respecting your body. A strong, healthy, happy body rewards you with incredible feelings of happiness and sensual pleasure. Isn't that reason enough to keep yourself fit?

◪   POWER TOOL 10

Do New Things

Take action. Change yourself. Travel, meet different types of people, pursue different things. Break your old habits and get out of ruts.

You will have to do new things to meet new people—go out to places you would never go before, with a friend or maybe even alone.

Stretch yourself. Discover new parts of yourself. Do new things, take risks, surprise yourself with new skills and abilities. Empower yourself by seeing that your old concepts of yourself were limiting you. Open up to the new.

We have many friends who have taken this advice all the way to doing things that they least wanted to do, or things that they most feared. Some have done very adventurous things like parachuting out of a plane, or perhaps walking on hot coals in one of the fire-walking workshops so popular nationwide.

But stretching yourself doesn't have to be that extreme; even a small stretch is really beneficial. Start by taking small risks, if you like. Wear something you never would have in the past, or go out to a different type of restaurant or nightclub than you normally would.

Put yourself in a position where you will meet new men or women. That's what Sophia did. She was a widow, a mother of five grown children. Still very youthful and vibrant, she had every intention of meeting and marrying again in her life.

Sophia took a job at a local newspaper, handling the "personal ads" column. For a year or so she diligently pasted up the column every week, watching the ads carefully and matching up people whenever she could. Then one day she received an ad in the mail that read: "Six ft. tall, blond Irishman. Likes to laugh and be outdoors. Let's have coffee and talk."

She read through the ad and said, "Hmmmmm," deciding right then and there to call the man herself. She dialed the phone and identified herself, and the two of them made a date for coffee.

The first coffee date lasted five hours. They sat in a diner and talked and talked. The second coffee date was the same. They had so much in common, so much to talk about. They still haven't run out of conversation because they were married last year and go out for coffee dates two or three times a week.

Sophia put herself in a position where she knew that she

would be able to meet lots of men, if she wanted to. After screening the mail for a long time, she was finally struck by the right one. She says that something just hit her when she read his ad. She knew that this man was the one for her. So she took action, called him, and the rest is happiness.

◪   POWER TOOL 11

Do It NOW!

Take action now because now is the moment of power. How much longer do you want to wait? Will you stumble through unfulfilling relationships and one-night stands? Or will you take the actions *now*, in the present?

"Someday my prince will come" might have worked for Sleeping Beauty, but why wait until "someday"? Take action now, in the present. Start the program; wake up and smell the coffee. Just do it! Start now to break the patterns that are holding you back in your relationships. Take the necessary actions, do the homework, use the exercises. If not now, when?

There is no such thing as the "past"; there is no such thing as the "future." These are just concepts that human beings have invented to organize the idea of time in our lives. All magic takes place in the present. All actions are taken at the moment. Each moment is precious and powerful. Don't let the moments of your life just drip away.

Seize the moment. Don't wait to live your life fully, and don't wait for life to serve itself to you on a silver platter. Take bold action in your life to create energy and movement and change. Now!

■ POWER TOOL 12

Model Your Desired Outcome

M*odeling* is a psychological term for mimicking or copying. It is a powerful technique for making changes in your life, used extensively in NLP (Neuro-Linguistic Programming) and other psychological and therapeutic technologies. To model is to copy, to imitate the behavior that you wish to develop in yourself.

Find a person who manifests the qualities you long for in your own life. Watch that person and notice how he or she does things. How does he stand? How does she walk, talk, or interact with people? How does he respond to life's challenges?

Begin to model that person's behavior as an experiment. If she smiles a lot, practice smiling a lot, too. This may feel uncomfortable and unnatural at the beginning, but remember, nothing changes unless you change first. Let yourself experiment with different responses. Be flexible!

Actors rehearse new characters, lines, and parts in movies and plays. Think of it in the same way; you are rehearsing for the results you want in your life.

There is nothing wrong with this. You are in the midst of personal transformation. You are molding yourself like a sculptor molds clay. You are taking the reins of your life. Instead of reacting to life's tests and challenges like a programmed robot, you are making conscious choices based on informed decisions.

Model the relationships that are powerful and loving in your life. Be aware of the qualities of relationships that are beautiful and loving, that you want to model in your own life.

Mary

. . . .

I used to watch two of my very dear friends, Paul and Diana von Welanetz, the creators and founders of The Inside Edge in

Southern California. They had been married twenty-five years and had the most wonderful marriage I could imagine.

I loved to see the way he held her arm as they walked, the way she would reach for his hand as they sat at a table together. The little tender things were the most impressive to me because they revealed an intimacy that I really wanted to bring to my next relationship.

Modeling them was a tremendous gift to me, and helped me become convinced that I deserved a beautiful, loving relationship like theirs. If they could do it, I could do it too.

If you want to learn about successful partnerships, look for relationships and partnerships that are working. Study them, model them. See the ways that the partners express intimacy, the levels of affection and respect they have for each other.

Watch the dynamics of their conversations, the way they communicate nonverbally. Notice the way they smile or talk. Try on the physical posture, walk around in their "moccasins" for a day. There is much to learn from modeling couples who are living the kind of relationship you long for.

Blessings

Think of a couple you know who seem to have a good relationship. Close your eyes and see the two of them in your imagination. Watch the happiness that they share as you say out loud or to yourself: "I love the way you are together," and "Thank you for being a good role model for the kind of love I am attracting into my life." It is a metaphysical truth that what you bless in others will•increase in your own life. Δ

■ POWER TOOL 13

Play Different Roles

As children we play and make believe. It is a natural ability of human beings to make up and invent, to create and manifest. The difference between make-believe, fantasy, or imagination and actual manifestation lies in the amount of commitment. Manifestation takes a commitment—the bigger the commitment, the better the results. Make a big commitment to attracting your ideal life mate in this physical reality, and be willing to receive it.

We all act out various roles in our own life drama. We all play the part of our personalities, our parents, and our beliefs. Like actors, rehearse the new roles that will help you achieve your goals. If you want to change your life, change your role.

There are many parts of you, many different selves or personalities. We think of these selves as the inner "board of director." Once you begin to acknowledge all these different parts of yourself, you will see how these parts might have conflicting goals and needs.

For example, the part of you that is young, sweet, and vulnerable must co-exist with the part of you that is a power-hungry business executive. The part of you that is the sex god or goddess might wage a war with the part of you that is prudish. In order to obtain any goal, it is necessary to get all the parts of you, or as many as possible, aligned toward achieving the same goal.

To attract your ideal life mate, you must coordinate and direct your different inner parts toward one powerful purpose. If you have a bunch of stray parts working against this goal, your chances of achieving it are minimized. These parts are highly capable of sabotaging the most wonderful goal or project if they are not aligned. So it is certainly to your advantage to get to know your inner "board of directors"—your various personalities—and convince them of the value of your goal.

Let's say that you have an inner part that wants to make lots of money. This part has driven you to achieving remarkable career goals, but whenever the idea of a love partnership is introduced, this part rebels. It might overwhelm you with negative thoughts about how you are too busy for a relationship, or remind you that you still have career goals that you haven't finished or that you will fail at your job. These horror thoughts could very easily sabotage a perfectly good relationship or keep you from ever attracting a suitable mate.

If you work with this part of yourself now, gearing it up for the fact that you have decided that you really must have a partner *now*, and that your work will suffer if you do *not* attract someone wonderful, you will be able to convince this rebellious part to help you attract a love partner.

Let's say a part of you is the "single and loving it" part. This part has been enjoying being single and having the option of many different exciting partners. This part is not at all happy about changing its life-style. Maybe this part will cause you to become too sexually demanding of a new partner, thus scaring the person off before a relationship has had a chance to flower.

Contact this part of yourself, and convince it of the pleasure that awaits with a monogamous relationship. If there was one trusted, safe partner, the levels of sensual pleasure and ecstasy could be heightened a thousandfold. With a built-in lover, the wasted time looking for and seducing new partners is replaced by total sexual bliss. What a better use of all that time and energy!

Board of Directors Scrapbook

Make a list of the different parts of yourself that you feel have a controlling and guiding effect on your life. Give these parts names and personalities. Maybe you call the sensual part of yourself Aphrodite, after the Greek goddess of love. Or maybe you call a part of yourself Wild Thing because it is kind of wild and untamed.

Have fun with this—after all, these are all parts of *you*. Once you have the list started, begin to save pictures from magazines that give you the same feelings as this part does. Maybe there is a wholesome, healthy part that you have named Sunshine, so you collect athletic pictures and images of summer.

Create a special "board of directors" scrapbook with pictures depicting each member of the board. This is an excellent way to get a clear, visual image of the various parts of you, so that you can begin to understand them and communicate with them.

If you feel that one of these parts of yourself is holding you back in your journey to meeting your ideal life mate, you can actually hold a conversation with this part. Here's how: Relax and sit in a comfortable position with the scrapbook in front of you. Leaf through the book as you say out loud, "Who would like to speak to me?" If your hand rests on a page, or you automatically turn to a page in the book, that's the part that you will consult.

Place the picture of the part of yourself in front of you. Close your eyes and ask, "What is it you want me to know?" Then just sit quietly and wait. Be patient. Soon you will get a visual picture, or hear a voice, or sense a feeling inside. Let yourself receive the message from this inner part of you wanting to communicate. When the message is received, say "Thank you for making your needs known to me." Δ

All the parts of yourself have one mission: to protect you, to ensure your happiness and survival. Each of them accomplishes this mission in the best way it knows how. When you realize this, you can honestly appreciate the different parts of yourself, and gently guide them into alignment with your goal of attracting your ideal life mate.

When each separate part is convinced that this new life mate will increase your happiness and increase your chances of survival, it will assist the process of attracting rather than blocking your flow of energy and mental focus.

You will feel better about yourself too, because these parts hold a lot of emotional and physical energy. Your self-esteem will continue to increase and you will feel happy to be who you are and blessed to be living the life you have.

After you have worked on yourself and achieved a high level of self-esteem and self-acceptance, you begin to feel very happy just to be who you are. You reach a point where you are feeling good about life, about your own growth, and you know that you are a good and worthy person who doesn't *need* a relationship to feel happy and fulfilled.

This is a magic time. This is when you will meet your ideal life mate.

If you like yourself, you may even have the confidence to go out on dates *alone*. Just take yourself to dinner, to a museum, to the park.

Sherrie is a woman who never would have considered going out by herself, without a woman friend as "protection." She was a single woman recovering from a very painful divorce. For the first year or two, she just worked on herself in therapy, in workshops, and counseling sessions to forgive and release her ex-husband. She wanted to release the anger so that she wouldn't blame the entire male population for the failings of her ex-husband.

In the third year, Sherrie had a real breakthrough, and she came to a new appreciation of her own strength and beauty. She stopped wanting a man to fulfill her; she stopped feeling that she *needed* a man to make her feel complete. She gave up trying to meet men and concentrated on her own career as a television producer.

Sherrie was invited to a book-signing party and she decided to go to the party alone. In the past she wouldn't have had the courage to admit she didn't have a date, and would have just stayed home alone. With her new strength and self-appreciation, however, she decided to attend the party by herself.

She had a great time at the event. She met two different men whom she spent time talking with during the evening. One of them asked for her phone number, and she gave it to him, thinking he just wanted to network with her about the television industry. She was very surprised when he called and asked her out to dinner. They went out on the first date, then the second, then a third and fourth and fifth. He wasn't like anyone she had ever dated (or married) before, and she knew that she had found her ideal life mate.

Sherrie had given up her anger, her neediness, and her search for a man to fulfill her. The benefits were incredible, and they doubled as she worked on herself. She became a happier person with more insight and self-understanding. Once she released the attachment and the need, she attracted her ideal life mate. They had a beautiful courtship and are now happily married.

Do new things. Take new actions. Make changes in your routine and your behavior. Travel to new places and meet new people. What have you got to lose except your limited definition of yourself?

7.

Activating the
Web of Love
with Visualizations
and Journaling

All world religions, no matter how ancient or modern, have a form of prayer or mental telepathy that allows for miracles to occur. Many religions and philosophies share the concept of a "web of life." Hinduism speaks of Indra's net, a fishing net strung with diamonds where each strand of the net intersects. Like strands of the net, human lives cross with others, creating diamonds of interactions and relationship where they intersect.

Ancient Hawaiian myths share stories of the web of Aka, or the beautiful spider, spinning the web of life. The spider spins and walks the web, but never gets caught in its own web. The web is sticky and dangerous to the hapless fly who gets caught, and even the occasional spider who slips and falls prey to its own web.

All human beings, all events, all aspects of life, are connected on the Aka web. Visualize it as a complex web of telephone lines that exist on an invisible level. The Aka web can be activated by playing the strings, or the Aka threads, with telepathic as well as physical techniques.

Use of ritual is one way to activate the Aka threads and send out a message. Other ways include meditation, journaling, writing, singing, prayer, visualization, affirmations, and invoking, or "calling" telepathically. In this book we share many techniques for developing the ability to activate the Aka web and fine-tune your ability to "call."

You can communicate with your life mate telepathically because you are connected. You can reach out to each other in meditation, in visualizations. You can play the Aka web strings that connect you the way an angel plays a harp. Always remember that nature is propelling you toward your ideal life mate because it serves the goals of nature.

◪   POWER TOOL 14

Visualization

Visualization is a term for a magical ability. To visualize, imagine, and create a picture in your mind, and then bring that vision into manifestation and fruition is nothing short of magic.

Visualization is actually a technique that uses the power of the mind to energize thoughts and activate them into reality. In essence, thought can attract to us that which we mentally embody.

Using visualizations is a "physics of manifestation" used for centuries by creative artists, ministers and clergy, politicians, and leaders. It can be considered a science that can be used to change and create new conditions of reality.

This phenomenal ability has been called many things, such as the power of prayer or spiritual mind treatment, mental focus, or using the power of the subconscious mind. Whatever you choose to call it, the ability is real and it can be tapped to attract your ideal life mate.

Thoughts are things. Everything you ever create in your life begins as a thought. Thoughts are the seeds that grow into reality, creating everything we have in our lives. Everything starts as an idea, and these thoughts become things.

Imagine your ideal relationship. Sense and feel it; enjoy the experience as a reality. Train your mind to hold the clear, unwavering picture of your ideal life mate. Do not allow doubt to creep in, or it will neutralize the activity.

Increase your ability to focus your thoughts on your goal of a wonderful life mate. Keep your focus and build a clear picture in your mind. Know and believe that this thought will grow to become that which you desire. Know that it will work. Omit all doubt.

Visualization Exercise

Read through your Five Qualities of Satisfaction and let an image of your ideal life mate form in your mind. See yourself with your partner, holding hands, looking into each other's eyes. Tune in to your feelings and your senses. What can you see, smell, hear?

Where are the two of you? Are you in a meadow, on a beach, in your living room? Focus on sharpening the picture of the two of you, holding hands and looking into each other's eyes. Let the feelings wash over you as you smile with happiness.

Visualize yourself clearly. Focus on this picture and know that this thought has power. It is a seed that you are planting in your consciousness. It is a step in the manifestation process. Trust the process, enjoy the feelings, and omit all doubt. Δ

■ POWER TOOL 15

Affirmation

What you have in life is the result of your beliefs, your subjective thought, and your words. Your words have power. They reveal what you are really thinking and what you really believe, and they are powerful tools for activating the web of love. Choose them carefully.

Affirmations use words to make statements of fact about what you want in life. Repeating these positive words energizes your subconscious mind.

Repetition is good. This is how you learn something new. Repeating something often fills your mind, and when your mind is focusing on something continually, that's what it will manifest.

We think 60,000 thoughts per day, 95 percent of them the same thoughts as we had yesterday. If you keep repeating something, it becomes part of your belief system. Once it is part of your belief system, you will create and manifest results from these beliefs.

When you create affirmations, use words that are close to what *you believe* are possible. This is the place to begin. Create expectation for effective affirmations, and know and believe they will work. Use words to focus. Plant good seeds in your mind. Thoughts and images are the seeds.

The universe will give you anything you want. You simply have to clear your own blocks to receiving it. Change yourself so that you can have what you want in your life.

Place your attention on finding your life mate. Keep this constantly in your mind and pay attention to it. Fill your mind and your being with the thoughts, exercises, and techniques in this book so that you keep your mind focused on this goal. Energy flows where your attention goes, and that is where the results show up.

Humans are moved by emotional energy. We react to excitement, enthusiasm, smiles, bliss, ecstasy, charisma, happiness, pleasure. These are motivational, positive desires. There is consensus that we humans have the potential to develop and explore untapped and unexplained talents and abilities. So, for even more powerful results using words and affirmations, add emotional energy to your words. Enthusiastically paint word pictures to create this emotional energy.

Affirmation Exercise

Affirmations are fun and easy to create. Start with short sentences that you can say many times during the day. For example, "I am attracting the perfect ideal life mate for me." Affirmations are stated as facts, with certainty.

You can write your own affirmations using your Five Qualities of Satisfaction. For instance, "I deserve a life mate who is _____" (fill in the blanks with your five qualities).

You can also put the written affirmations all over your house, taped to your bathroom mirror, in the kitchen, and wherever you spend a lot of time. Repetition is the way the brain learns new things, so repeat your affirmations often during the day. Δ

◪ POWER TOOL 16

Treatment and Prayer

Prayer and spiritual mind treatment are ways of focusing your mind while asking for the power of God, the Universal Life Force, or whatever else you call the divine power that is our source to attract, manifest, or bring into being that which the prayer is requesting.

Prayer is a form of affirmation and visualization, fueled with faith and belief, further intensified by the addition of emotional energy and spiritual fervor. No wonder prayer is so powerful for so many! Miracles happen all the time through the power of prayer.

Here is a treatment, or prayer, for attracting your ideal life mate, friend, and lover. It is inspired by Ernest Holmes, founder of the New Thought and Science of Mind churches.

> Love in me is unified with Love in all. Universal Love is now attracting into my life all love, joy, and partnership. I am one with all lovers, with love relationships, with all life. As I listen in the silence, the voice of all humanity sings to me and listens to my call.
>
> The great Love which I now feel for my life mate is the universal Love. I give Love and therefore I have abundant Love. I give, therefore I receive. I inspire, therefore I am inspired. I am now surrounded by all Love, all partnership, all companionship, all health, all happiness, all success. I AM ONE WITH LOVE. I smile in the silence while the great spirit bears this message to the whole world.

■ POWER TOOL 17

Maoli

The Hawaiian word *maoli* means "to bring into existence." Don uses a technique based on this concept every day as part of his morning beach walk and meditation. He has created very powerful results in his business as well as his love life by using visualization techniques.

Don visualizes exactly what he wants in his life and sees it on the horizon. He gazes out to sea, pinpointing a spot on the horizon, and clearly imagines what it is he wants to create in his life. He spends time perfecting each detail of the visualization because it is much easier to correct something before it happens than to deal with problems later.

This is a form of intense planning, but it also awakens the deep subconscious mind and engages it in the planning activity. The meditative stance creates a light trance.

When the conscious mind is in a trance, it becomes open to suggestion. The mind grabs on to the image that is being visualized on the horizon, and receives the message that this is important information. The mental image is imprinted deeply on the inner mind, and this activates a number of both right and left brain connections. The left side of the brain begins to act, inventing solutions and ways to take action on the imprinted command. The right side of the brain begins to activate the Aka web.

We teach the Maoli technique in our advanced "Finding Each Other" workshop. Jana, a woman in her late forties with several grown children, was really impressed with the rituals and techniques she learned in the training. She actively used them after the workshop was over, rising at dawn to do the Maoli technique, gazing at the horizon and visualizing her ideal life mate coming into her life. She did not want to have to travel to find him; she wanted him to come right into her life.

Jana avidly practiced her techniques for several months, every morning at dawn. Then one day, her roommate answered a phone call from one of her ex-boyfriends, who was calling to ask her out. She told him she felt that their relationship was long completed, but she had a friend he might like to meet.

She put Jana on the phone, and the two struck an immediate connection. Jana made plans to meet the man and they fell head over heels in love. He was everything she had asked for in her list of five qualities, and when we last heard from her she was in the middle of a major romance.

Jana used the techniques and her Five Qualities of Satisfaction as a guide, and never had to leave her house to meet this man! This true story illustrates the magic that happens every day. Anything is possible!

Here's another example, from our own experience.

Don

Don is a very romantic man. He would walk on the beach at his home in Hawaii and see honeymoon couples embrace, walk hand in hand, and kiss in the moonlight. As he watched the happy couples, he longed for a woman who could share the beauty and romance he observed in others. This sense of longing and desire for emotional connection set up a chain of events that eventually produced the exact outcome he wanted.

He would visualize the qualities he wanted in a woman, seeing her grow clearer on the horizon every day. He did not get specific in the visualization about physical body type or hair color. He visualized the inner qualities and feelings that the woman would have. He wanted someone who was physical and athletic, who was romantic and passionate, who was spiritual and committed to teaching or inspiring others, and who had a business sense or level of ambition and ability that would resonate with his. Every morning he meditated on these qualities, and the desire for this relationship grew.

He also worked on himself every day, increasing his own self-esteem and inner strength, convincing himself that he deserved the best. You can only have as much happiness as your inner self feels it deserves, so he worked to increase his ability to deserve the best. After about a year of this visualizing and calling out, the Aka web was activated enough to bring the two of us together.

Meanwhile, in California, Mary was singing, dancing, and creating rituals that would set up an emotional charge and send out her own "calling" into the universe.

Mary was activating the web on her end of the thread. Don was activating the web on his end of the thread. When we came together we were amazed at the synchroneity of our journeys toward finding each other. Many times we found, by backtracking and checking our calendars, that we were doing intense emotional work on ourselves and activating the web at *the same time.*

☑ POWER TOOL 18

Music

Music is another way to activate the web of life and love connections. Love songs touch the deepest part of a person's inner soul, haunting the lonely recesses of the heart. One need only listen to the popular music on any station, from country to classical, from rap to rock and roll, to hear love songs dominating the airwaves.

The most common way that humans communicate love, romance, loss of love, breaking up, or falling in love is through music. It is actually quite difficult to write and speak about love. But music touches us in ways that words can't, and opens our hearts to feel the emotions in us.

Music is such a wonderful gift. Songs connect us directly with our emotions. We learn the words and sing in our cars or in the shower, the words going straight to our hearts. Love songs can be beautiful celebrations of joy or poignant lessons in loss. Music wakes up the emotions and floods the spirit with a symphony of feelings.

One of the ways we found each other was through music. When we traced back, we discovered that we had both been listening to love songs and romantic music exclusively. This really didn't make sense considering that we were both alone at the time. Nevertheless, we felt drawn to listen to very romantic, even sappy, love songs.

We have discovered that the power of music can be used to attract your ideal life mate and to get you into the mood for love. In our workshops we play tapes of love songs as background music, and we have a beautiful tape we constantly play at home just to enjoy the feelings of love and romance it evokes.

Here are a few songs that are very powerful for healing and for activating the web. Sing them to yourself. Try singing them while looking at yourself in the mirror, taking a shower, and driving in the car, or hum them in your mind as you go through your day.

All of these love songs are to be sung *to yourself* originally, as a form of self-healing and love. Then imagine that you are playing and singing them to your life mate, who is waiting somewhere at the other end of the web.

SONGS OF LOVE AND LONGING

"Devoted to You," by Carly Simon and James Taylor

"In My Life," by the Beatles

"I'm Calling You," from the movie *Baghdad Cafe*

"You Bring Me Joy," sung by Anita Baker

"The Greatest Love," sung by Stevie Wonder or Whitney Houston

"Love Me Tender," sung by Elvis Presley

"You Are So Beautiful," sung by Joe Cocker

These are some of the love songs that we have found to be particularly useful. You can use any music that evokes feelings of joy, self-esteem, happiness, appreciation for your life, and so on.

Music unlocks the emotions and is the doorway to the heart. It can melt away past hurts, if you allow it to, and bring new freshness and hope.

◪ POWER TOOL 19

Keeping a Journal

We recommend keeping a journal as you embark on the journey of self-healing. You can use this journal in many ways: to write down your dreams, to work out frustrations and questions in your life, and to activate the web of love.

There are many ways a journal can be used. One way is to write out all your feelings about the processes in this book; another is to write about your past loves in an attempt to sort them out and learn from them. Yet another way is to tap into your inner self by using your nondominant hand to write.

This technique opens up some parts of the inner you that may surprise you. Often, the voice that emerges from the nondominant hand in journaling exercises is very young and childlike. This young version of you expresses its needs and hurts, opinions and joys, in a very special way. Try the following technique in your journal.

Nondominant Hand Journaling

On a blank sheet of paper in your journal, draw a line dividing the paper from top to bottom. At the top of the page, write

"Reasons my past relationships didn't work." With your dominant hand, make a list in the left column of at least ten reasons.

Now switch the pen to your other hand and let your nondominant hand write its opinion in the right column next to the reasons previously given. You will probably be amazed at what the other hand has to say!

This exercise illustrates the point we have made many times in this book: you have many inner parts, members of your inner "board of directors." Some of them may have a very different opinion of the way you are conducting your life than your conscious mind thinks! It is valuable to check in with these inner parts as often as possible to make sure that they are not sabotaging your efforts toward success in all aspects of your life, including finding an ideal life mate. Δ

You may also use your journal in conjunction with the inner journeys, visualizations, and meditations that are shared in many of the chapters of this book. After you have listened to the meditations, write in your journal about all the new insights, symbols, and messages you received.

Mary
· ·

I was keeping a very active journal. It seemed that poetry and thoughts just poured out of me during this year-long period of time. I felt haunted by the evocative love songs, the fire mythology of Pele, the legends of gods and goddesses, and the sensuous beauty of Hawaii, and I found myself returning there three times in one year.

The following selection, taken from my journal, written at the exact same period of time that Don was doing the daily Maoli technique, reflects the intensity of my emotional search. The energy aspects of calling, longing, and invocation are apparent in the excerpt and therefore we include it as a sample of the emotional and sexual energy that was needed to attract each other as the life mates of our dreams.

My own path is certainly taking a Goddess- or nature-based form. The female creative force fills me with true ecstasy. I love the commitment to living rituals and I want to be a part of an ongoing group that creates and acts out rituals consistently. The living ritual is such a part of my soul ... that is why I love drama and theatre and dance ... that is why I devoted the first part of my life to theatre ... the living experience of human drama ... of the compacted essential life force. ...

Theatre is totally spiritual in its truest forms. The origins of theatre are the same as the origins of religion ... Storytelling and wonder ... nature and the gods. Reenacting tales of the hunt ... the shaman journey ... the lessons from above ... and below.

So the Goddess calls with increasing urgency. She fills me with sadness about not being in Kauai ... she drives me to read more and more books ... she asks me to find others like myself and join with them in song and dance.

She asks me to find a high priest to make love with ... a man of equal stature and power to mine to invoke the Goddess and God in sexual ecstasy ... for the purpose of healing the planet ... healing ourselves ... connecting with the life force. She has cooled my rampant wanderings and made me look deeply into myself ... to honor my power ... to honor hers. The sexual searching phase is ended ... it actually ended long ago ... and I have been healing myself and my past sexual and marriage alliances. ...

I embrace the Priestess ... the time has come for me to really serve. I own my sexual power and hold it for myself ... for the healing of myself and others ... I promise to use this awesome and enormous gift wisely ... to make sure to take care of myself ... to love and be loved.

*   *   *

Writing is therapeutic and freeing. As you write, just let your creativity flow onto the empty pages. You will be amazed to look back at the pages of poetry, sketches, and insightful writing that come forth when you let yourself go. The journal is a place to release emotions and passions, to explore inner images, to record spiritual awakenings.

It is very rewarding to let your sexual fantasies grow into poetry, journaling, and song. Your journal is also an excellent place to explore this type of writing.

This idea introduces a very special and engaging aspect to sexuality—the power of images and fantasy. By *fantasy*, we do not mean the fantasies that men's magazines proffer. We are referring to an inner imaging closely aligned to dreaming, an ability to let the mind wander through colors, scenes, and entire movies rich in personal meaning for lovers.

This ability to fantasy-dream is the connection among sexuality, spirituality, and creativity. Just as a poet or a painter uses his or her talent to bring forth a work of literary or visual art, you create a new kind of art during the experience of sexual connection.

Write about your sexual love! Paint, draw, sing, and dance for the joy of it. Making love is the ultimate art form. Bring it into other forms by letting your creativity flow. The journal is an excellent place to explore this type of poetry and drift-writing.

8.

Ceremonies to Activate the Magic of Love

This chapter is about magic—the magic of love and life and dreams that come true, the magic of finding a lover and partner who can really communicate and connect with you, the magic of lost lovers reunited across time and space.

We believe in magic. There is really no other way to describe the beauty and exhilaration of connecting with a true love; it is simply magic. And it is magic that can be tapped and used to heal yourself, to attract a true love and to enhance the quality of the relationship you create together.

We are living examples of the fact that it is never too late to find your life mate and perfect partner. We had both been through many relationships and a few marriages. We feel now that those earlier relationships were a training ground, like a glorious rehearsal for the magnificent love that awaited us.

There is no explanation for love or magic. People meet and fall in love every day—that is magic. Babies are born and huge trees grow from tiny seeds. There is a life force that fuels and fills us, that motivates our grandest passions and accomplishments, that drives us onward on the journey of life. Along that journey we meet many people, and they teach us the lessons we need to learn. We move on, following the adventure of our personal and spiritual evolution. It is a quest for knowledge, for healing, for wholeness, for love.

What's different about our approach to love and relationships is that we draw from a human-potential, shamanistic, metaphysical, and magical background in the tools and techniques we share. We have learned about love and relationships by experience and by experimentation. We have both studied many forms of healing, self-help, and personal growth techniques, transformational and shamanic concepts, and spiritual paths. We met through the exploration of Huna, the ancient Polynesian system of healing and magic. Many of the techniques we apply and share are based on Huna philosophy. Huna is a system of love, friendship, and blessing, of warmth, appreciation, and openness. It is where the famous concept of Aloha Spirit originated.

The magic concepts in this chapter are not strange or spooky. Shamanism is not anything to be afraid of. The word *shaman* means "healer," and we are using the healing techniques of shamanic systems to help others create successful love relationships.

We have found that these techniques work for healing the past and opening a person up to love. They certainly worked for us in our own relationship; we found each other using these techniques. They have worked for many others who have taken our workshops and have used our methods.

We have a heartfelt commitment to teaching and sharing all we know that might be healing or useful to others. It is part of our shared life purpose together, to bring inspiration and happiness to others and to share the love and beauty of the Aloha Spirit. And now we invite you to help us create an atmosphere of magic, of love and healing, of appreciation and excitement, of thankfulness, blessing, and celebration.

As children we knew that the world was a magical place. There was magic all around us and miracles everywhere. Remember in *Peter Pan*, when Tinker Bell was very sick and in order to bring her back to life we all clapped our hands and chanted, "I *do* believe in fairies ... I DO believe in fairies"?

How many of you clapped with all your might to bring Tinker Bell back?

Magic. The unexplainable, mysterious spark of enchantment that makes dreams come true, that brings lovers together from distant parts of the planet, turns the Wicked Witch into stone and the Cinder Girl into a princess.

Our cultural heritage is full of references to magic of all sorts. We have fairy godmothers, fairy princesses, magic wands, magic spells, pixie dust, wizards and dragons, and enchanted forests. Teenagers are fascinated with games such as Dungeons and Dragons; children play with space fantasy figures and magical animals.

Some of the largest-grossing movies of our generation have been *Star Wars*, *Star Trek*, E.T., and other futuristic space fantasies. These movies are full of rich mythology and magic occurrences. We are moved by these films, deeply affected by the power, emotion, and heroism. They are epic dramas that enchant us, and our children go back to see them over and over again. Why?

Because they call to us. They pull at our hearts and souls; they speak to a very deep place in every human being that longs for connection—a place that remembers the magic.

This is where love lives. To open up to love is to return to innocence, to romance, to believing in magic. We invite you to become innocent and trusting, to open your heart to love and magic.

Know that in order for the magic to work, you have to really want it. First, you have to believe that it is possible; second, you must know in your heart of hearts that you deserve love; and third, you must *ask* for your ideal life mate in your life *now*.

CEREMONIES

Our culture celebrates the major rituals of life with ceremony—song and dance, food and wine, flowers and laughter. Human beings love rituals; we respond emotionally and physically to repetition, music, and rhythm. This is because rituals are predictable; we find it comforting and soothing to know what is going to happen next.

Birthdays, Christmas, and most other holidays are rituals that families share every year. Even funerals are powerful shared ritual experiences where loved ones grieve, embrace, eat, drink, and share the loss of one they loved. Every culture has rituals that bind and unite people. Throughout history, rituals have been created to celebrate birth, entrance into manhood or womanhood, marriage, and death. Or a ritual might be something as simple as making coffee in the same way each day, brushing your teeth at the same time every morning, driving the same roads to get to work.

Rituals are not for everyone. They have a profound effect when used by people who have faith and belief in them; otherwise they are just silly sounds and movements. If you find that you are not attracted to the concepts and techniques in this chapter, or if they strike you as strange or uncomfortable in any way, move on to other techniques in this book. Use the tools that you can relate to so they will be effective for *you*.

We offer a large variety of techniques for attracting your life mate, so don't worry if some of them do not appeal to you. One reason we have included such a variety of experiences is so there will be "something for everyone." For example, Mary has had extremely positive results using rituals in her work with individual clients. Don is more attracted to visualizations and deep inner work.

Rituals are very powerful because they take us away from our day-to-day lives and create a moment or event that stands out. Ceremonies and rituals such as high school graduation, weddings, and funerals all share the same elements: they stir our emotions, they are theatrical and dramatic, they engage our attention and our senses, they create a sense of awe and wonder, and they stand out in our memories.

All the world's religions draw upon ceremony and ritual to create a sense of spiritual connection and celebration. By engaging the emotions and physical senses, by asking participation in acts of power and reverence, by creating a special moment set apart from the rest of life, rituals create an opportunity for new attitudes, new thoughts and behavior, new inspiration to break through to one's consciousness.

The Catholic Church has used these basic principles for almost two thousand years. In masses and ceremonies filled with ritual, stylized gestures, foreign language, chants and hymns, and power objects such as candles, incense, special robes and altars, the church has created a sense of awe and wonder, reverence and mystery.

WHY DO RITUALS WORK?

Rituals work because they deeply impress the subconscious mind. They convince your subconscious that you are really serious about wanting something in your life. A ritual operates emotionally and physically, sending strong messages to the brain that you mean business.

In his wonderful book *Urban Shaman*, Serge Kahili King explains ritual as "consciously organized behavior intended to impress and influence." He feels that an effective ritual ought to leave a lasting impression and strongly influence people to change attitudes, assumptions, or expectations. A ritual must be intellectually and emotionally satisfying, and the best use is for healing and the enhancement of positive behavior and positive change.

In *Spiral Dance* by Starhawk, the author says that a ritual is designed to raise power and to influence or direct the flow of energy. Everything is interconnected, and every action creates reaction in the ever-spiraling flow of energy. She goes on to say that energy is essentially love, and love is magic.

Our experience with rituals has been dramatic. We have experienced their power and magic, and we have seen them work changes in attitudes and expectations.

The most effective rituals make use of all the senses and stir the emotions. They harness the energy of the senses and the emotions, combined with physical gestures and movements, fueled with the power of belief. If you place your belief in something, you give it the power to work.

This is not some outside power at work; rituals are not scary or weird. You are the one who empowers the ritual or the ceremony. The power, energy, and ability comes from you and moves through your body and mind. But if you doubt or ridicule the activity, it will probably not work effectively for you.

Ideally, a ritual is a multisensory emotional and physical experience, performed at the same time, in the same place. It is approached with an attitude of vulnerability and humility, an acknowledgment of openness to advice and input. Emotions are generated, and there is a feeling of communion and connection with nature and all of life.

CREATING YOUR OWN RITUALS

The types of rituals you can create are based entirely on your personal likes and dislikes, and the power of your creative imagination. Rituals can be silly or funny, deeply serious and significant, or breezy and light. This is the fun part—there is no right or wrong way.

In our workshops, we use rituals in the healing process. Often groups of participants create rituals as part of the workshop format. One ritual in particular stands out in our memories because it was so creative and irreverent, yet powerful and effective at the same time.

A group of four people in the workshop created a ritual that had elements of rap music, a section that was like the old Supremes and Temptations dance routines, with Motown-style choreography and do-wop background music. It was absolutely hilarious and delightful, and very powerful, too.

Another ritual expressed the need to create and manifest a career change. The basic chant in the seven-step ritual was "Get a Job, Sha-Na-Na; Get a Job, Sha-Na-Na" as the group rattled and drummed along; pretty soon everyone was chanting "Get a Job, Sha-Na-Na."

Rituals are very creative and satisfying to perform. Usually they are done all alone in the privacy of your home, or with a small group of trusted friends. It is fun and freeing to create this way, so let your imagination go and have a great time!

Here are the seven steps to creating a ritual:

1. Bless the space

2. Honor nature, the directions, and the Life Force

3. Sing, dance, pray, meditate

4. Ask for guidance, a sign, or an omen

5. Send healing energy

6. Give thanks

7. Close the space

Explanation of the Steps

Step 1. Bless the space. Inscribe a circle in the air or draw a shape on the ground. Bring your personal, emotional, and spiritual energy into the space. Dedicate the space to the creation of a special experience. Declare the space to be safe and protective.

Step 2. Honor nature, the directions, and the Life Force. Honor the elements and forces in nature by naming them: Fire, Water, Earth, and Air. In many medicine systems, the four directions have special energy and represent different qualities.

In Native American rituals, North means strength, wisdom, spirit, and intuition; the color for North is white. South is trust and innocence; the color is red. East is illumination, the rising sun and the sacred clown; the color is yellow. West is introspection, the sacred dream, death and rebirth; the color is black. The colors are used in the creation of prayer flags that are tied on string, sewn into large banners, and worn as part of ceremonial costuming. The colors black, white, yellow, and red are used most often because of their meaning and symbolism.

In ancient European systems, however, North means the earth and the body, South is fire and energy, East is air and the mind, and West is water and the emotions. There are no particular colors associated with the directions in Western systems.

We share these meanings as a reference point for you, but it is perfectly all right to invent your own colors, meanings, and directions in your rituals and ceremonies. It is a personal, creative, and beautiful experience to create a ritual. You can invent your own meanings for each of the directions or use an existing system.

Step 3. Sing, dance, pray, meditate. This is the "active" step of the ritual. It is important to *do* something active and physical in the space. Dancing is wonderful; chanting or singing is very effective, too. Prayer or meditation can be done during this step also. You can energize the space by mentally surrounding it with love, magic, and creativity. Song and dance, use of smudging and smoke, drumming, ritualized or stylized movements and gestures are all effective because they engage and involve the senses.

Step 4. Ask for guidance, a sign, or an omen. In this step you make a request by asking for guidance and advice. Your answer may come in the form of a sign or omen. Be aware of the activity around you as you perform this step in the ritual.

We do not believe in negative omens. We choose to see all signs, portents, and omens as positive signs. We have the power to choose, so why not choose the positive?

Very powerful omens could be right under your nose; you must look for them and be awake. Once, when asking for guidance, Mary saw a huge rainbow burst through the clouds. Another time a huge owl flew past us while we were asking for guidance about an upcoming project; we took that as a very positive sign.

Step 5. Send healing energy. If there is a person or situation you would like to see improved, this is the time to send some healing energy. Focus your intention to send the energy, and it will be done. You can sit still or move around. The important part is to think of the person with love and send healing energy force to them.

For example, you might visualize this healing force as a beam of light, or a ray of sunshine, or a wall of positive energy. You can send colored light to symbolize various types of healing, or to isolate body parts; or send a field of colored, golden, pink, or white light. This is very personal, as are all elements of your ritual. Do what feels the best and most powerful. Follow your intuition.

Generate energy and send it out with loving intent to help

and improve the quality of people's lives. By inviting love, beauty, and energy that is positively charged, you can become the conduit for an encounter that is profound for whomever you are healing as well as for yourself.

Step 6. Give thanks. Sincerely thank all of the forces and elements for assisting in the ritual. You may personalize this energy as angels, gods and goddesses, or power animals.

Give thanks with all your heart; feel grateful for all the blessings in your life. Acknowledge the good around you and bless it.

Step 7. Close the space. Reverse the process you used at the beginning of the ritual. If you opened the space by inscribing a circle or shape to hold the space, undo the circle or bubble this time. Say, "I close this space and return it to its previous state. Let all the good that has been created here today go forth into the world with my love and blessings. Amen" (or "So be it," or "And so it is," or whatever you prefer). Leave the space and go on with your life.

When you first start out, you may want to follow these guidelines. Keep in mind that these are steps we created, and you are more than welcome to invent your own. Rituals are completely personal, and you can create them any way you want.

This sequence has been effective for our uses, but feel free to change or delete any steps you want to after you get into performing your own rituals.

POWER OBJECTS AND RITUAL TOOLS

Wands and Staffs

Wands and staffs are often used in rituals to focus and send energy. The wand is a powerful tool; it can make a laser beam of power and energy out of an otherwise vague energetic field.

Power objects are powerful only if you believe they are. The wand can be a stick you find on the beach, or it can be a beautifully tooled, hand-crafted piece of fine jewelry.

Wands and staffs are nice to hold onto during a ritual or ceremony. They seem to lend a feeling of comfort to the leader, and act as a symbol of power to the participants. The wand acts as a pointer, determining the directions as the leader calls them out, and it can send energy out into the desired location in the universe. Wands and staffs are effective in opening and closing the space.

Early in her life-mate manifestation process, Mary created two wands to use in rituals. One was to represent the yin, or feminine aspects; the other represented the yang, or masculine forces. She decorated two 25-inch sticks with soft suede, beads, feathers, fringe, and amulets that had meaning for her.

The feminine wand was a pinkish mauve and the amulets were small silver angels and crescent moons and stars. The masculine wand was created in shades of forest green and purple, with beaded Native American crescents and designs decorating it. At the end of each wand she attached a medium-size crystal. She used these wands in many private rituals to call to her life mate. It was soothing and powerful to hold one in each hand and wave them across each other in dancelike gestures. She has not used them for any other type of ceremony since, and they now are mounted on a wall in Hawaii. They served the purpose they were created for, and they are retired to a place of respect and reverence.

Crystals and Stones

Crystals have had enormous publicity and popularity in recent years. There are many books about crystals that praise their beauty and healing power. Whether you believe they can heal and communicate or not, they are very beautiful and are pleasing to the subconscious and the eye.

Crystals look nice when placed on an altar or in a circle around the ritual space. You can use a crystal to symbolize a quality you are asking for in your life or in your life mate, or to meditate upon as part of the ceremony. A crystal could be held in each hand as a way of "grounding yourself," and you might imagine the color of your crystal entering and relaxing you.

Mary has a nice collection of crystals and uses them in her meditations and rituals—mostly for their aesthetic appeal, but also because she feels they lend a focusing power to the experience.

Smudging

Smudging with smoke is a useful tool in creating rituals and ceremonies, in blessing a space, and in clearing out negative energy. The burning of sage or cedar, or even incense, has a powerful effect on the body and the mind. Smoke takes a ritual to a deeper level and impresses the subconscious mind. This is why the Catholic Church uses incense, Buddhists have joss sticks and incense burning constantly in the temples, and Native Americans burn pitch and sage.

Smoke is beautiful to watch as it wafts and curls. It is mesmerizing and induces a light trance state. It is magical looking and it smells good. There is also the element of potential danger. Fire recalls a deep animal fear, and the harnessing of fire is a human triumph. Use smoke and smudging in your rituals outside. Be careful if using it inside; you will probably set off your smoke alarm! Use small amounts, since too much is overkill.

CHANTS, PERCUSSION, AND SOUND EFFECTS

Chants, sound effects, rattles, and drums are used extensively in rituals. The physical body and the emotional self react strongly to music and sound effects. Percussion instruments create a steady beat that allows the body to fall into a light trance, making it even more open and vulnerable to input at a deep subconscious level.

If you feel that you would enjoy such sound effects in your own rituals, you may want to purchase a selection of rattles, gourds, or drums. These are available in music stores and ethnic arts shops. Import stores or primitive and folk art specialty shops may carry authentic shamanic rattles from Africa or South America. The selection of this type of instrument is highly personal, as is any power object or tool. Let your intuition allow you to select the perfect set of instruments.

Mary went through a phase a few years ago when she was powerfully attracted to various percussion instruments. She sought out specialty and primitive import stores, buying rattles from Native American tribes, Mexican tourist shops, Hawaiian hula schools, and import stores specializing in folk arts from South America. She used these rattles and drums in many group chants and rituals, and even kept a rattle in her car to create spontaneous chants while stuck in traffic. She had miraculous positive results in "rattling" for a parking space, rattling for the successful signing of a script contract, and rattling for her life mate.

In creating an effective ritual you must charge the environment and your own consciousness with excitement and intention. You can chant, rattle, sing, make physical movements, or dance. The more you activate and involve your body and emotions, the more powerful the results will be.

HOW TO CREATE A SHRINE

Creating a shrine or altar is a lot of fun. A shrine brings a focal point to a ritual; it's like the stage, and the action takes place in front of it.

A shrine can be anything: a rock, a fireplace mantle, a table in the corner, or a patch of grass. It is your attention that grants significance and meaning to the altar. If you declare that a spot is an altar or shrine, it is.

We create altars all the time, usually for our books or other writing projects underway. We place flowers, candles, a couple of crystals, and a picture of ourselves looking very happy around the shrine with the manuscript in the middle. It's fun. It makes us excited about the project, and we charge it up with our joy.

TWO MAJOR TYPES OF RITUALS

Usually, rituals are used either for healing a person or a situation, or to manifest changes in the physical world. We have divided the rituals in this chapter into these two sections. The first are for healing yourself, your friends, the planet, or anything else you want to apply them to. This section includes a powerful set of rituals for healing divorce. The second section are rituals to use for manifesting physical changes in your life.

If you are interested in healing your past loves, start on the first section. If you want to skip over the healing rituals and go straight to the manifestation rituals, feel free to do so.

Healing Rituals

Here are a few rituals that we invented to assist the healing, releasing, and forgiveness processes. Several were created to allow clients and workshop participants to get in touch with and let go of personal issues. Most of them just come naturally from inner guidance, though some were actively created to address a specific area that needed attention.

BASIC HEALING RITUAL
This is a basic ritual that is great for healing past loves, family members or friends, the planet, or a situation in the news. It can be performed alone or in a group.

Step 1. Consecrate the space by drawing a circle (clockwise) with a knife, shaman staff, or magic wand. Say the following:

> I consecrate this circle for the purpose
> of honoring the God and Goddess in all of us—
> to send love and healing energy, to respect
> the yin and yang forces, to dance in
> the light of love.

Step 2. Light cedar or smudge stick, and smoke the area to cleanse it. Honor the directions or elements.

Step 3. Sing a song or chant or speak a spontaneous prayer. Create an altar to the four elements—Fire, Water, Earth, and Air—and decorate it with flowers and candles. If desired, place images of those whom you intend to heal, or the situation you want to heal, on the altar. Lay out power objects such as crystals, flowers, wands, and any other desired symbolic representations.

Step 4. Ask for guidance. Pray, meditate.

Step 5. Begin ceremonies.

Ceremony to Heal Ourselves: Meditate on the healing that you want in your life.

Ceremony to Heal Our Families and Loved Ones: Send love and light to family members one at a time. Speak their names out loud softly; rattle, sing, and chant if you feel like it.

Ceremony to Heal the Planet: Send healing energy through your hands to various locations on the planet. Speak prayers silently or out loud, send light and love.

Step 6. Give thanks.

Step 7. Undo the magic circle by moving the knife, staff, or wands in the opposite direction (counterclockwise). Close the ceremony by blessing God, the Goddess, and the Life Force.

WATERFALL RITUAL

This waterfall ritual was invented as a way to release the past, celebrate rebirth, and cleanse the spirit. Water is very healing and soothing. It is also a metaphor for rebirth and baptism. You can use a waterfall, a pond, a swimming pool, the ocean, a lake, or even the bathtub or shower in your home.

Start by blessing the space and asking for the power to bless and release.

Next, get a clear picture in your mind of what you are willing to let go of and release. Perhaps it is your attachment to past hurts, or your tendency to become jealous. Whatever, get a strong, clear feeling and let the pain of that quality build up a bit inside.

When you have built up the emotional content, plunge yourself into the water and let it go. Release, forgive, and really let go in a big way. The more dramatic you make this, the more it will impress your subconscious body. Dunk yourself under the water and splash. Step under the waterfall or shower; let the water wash away the pain and memories of that feeling. Let the hurt go and let yourself drift in the soft vulnerability of the water.

Now think of a quality or blessing with which you would like to replace the old feeling. Perhaps it is compassion, or understanding, or unconditional love. Let that new quality fill in the spaces inside yourself where the old quality was. Let it fill you and enrich you as the water washes over your body.

Breathe deep, relax, and give thanks. Then step out of the water, dry yourself off, and thank the space and the element of water for the profound blessing that it offers.

DIVORCE AND SEPARATION RITUALS

Rituals and ceremonies are very powerful healing tools. It is actually possible to sing and chant your ex-love out of your life.

Divorce and separation are the only major events in life not blessed and celebrated with ritual and ceremony. It is considered a painful humiliation to be borne alone, crying into your pillow or in the presence of therapists and close friends. It is not celebrated, it is not blessed, it is not enjoyed. We believe that this can change. It is time to consider a new form of divorce and separation.

Here are a few rituals invented to assist the separation and divorce releasing process. In each case, you may open and close the space in whatever way you choose. We include just the middle section, the content or meat of the ritual.

1. *Reclaiming the space ritual*. One of the first rituals to do after a separation is to reclaim the space. If you have moved out and are setting up a new home or apartment, be especially aware that this is *your* new space. You decide how to decorate, what to keep and what to throw out, what colors reflect the new you, and what environment is the most supportive to your healing process.

If your spouse moves out, you have an altogether different set of challenges. It is time to reclaim and rebless the space. Approach this process with reverence. Begin your ritual by honoring the elements or the directions, then move to the next step.

First, clean out, organize, or throw out anything that reminds you of painful experiences. This includes furniture, books and files, ugly posters and paintings, and plants that recall the past. Put all pictures away in photo albums and stick them in the cupboard. There is no reason to reopen old wounds by looking at pictures of happier days. It's time to start fresh and get on with your new life.

2. *Paint ritual* (Mary's story). After my ex-husband moved out of the house I wanted to reclaim the space for myself and my new life. I decided to repaint and redecorate my kitchen and living room. I invited eight of my female friends over (also my brother and my mother) for a painting party. I supplied the brunch, champagne, paint, and other supplies. They worked and sang our theme song (tune of "I'm Gonna Wash That Man Right Outa My Hair" from *South Pacific*):

I'm gonna paint that man
Right outa my house

I'm gonna paint that man
Right outa my house

I'm gonna paint that man
Right outa my house
And send him on his way!

It was a lot of fun and my house looked beautiful after a few hours of hard work. I have thought about that day, and the love and support I received from my friends, every time I look at the walls of the kitchen and living room. We painted it lovely shades of apricot and off-white that look absolutely gorgeous in the morning light.

After the painting party, I bought a couple of pieces of furniture, some accent pieces, new pillows, and some new plants. The place was transformed and suddenly it really felt like *my home*. I fell in love with the house, and it was my sanctuary during the process of separation and divorce. It could have been a painful memory of my past marriage but, instead, it became a powerful healing environment. One of my woman friends called it the "Love Cottage" because she was positive that I was constantly entertaining helpless men and luring them into my boudoir. The truth is, it was a Love Cottage because I really began to experience self-love in that house.

3. *Lysol ritual.* A friend shared her story of reclaiming her space. She said that after her unfaithful husband moved out, she ritually scoured all the walls and ceilings of the house with Lysol. She paid particular attention to the bedroom, and felt 100 percent better afterwards. The Lysol is a metaphor for cleansing and renewing the space, and hard scrubbing and cleaning are healthy ways to blow off a lot of steam and vent pent-up hostility. One of the major forms of therapy for our mothers' generation was heavy

cleaning. Try it sometime if you haven't already. Clean with a vengeance, and you'll feel a lot better afterwards.

4. *Smoke blessing—smudging the environment.* Another ritual for reclaiming your space comes from a Native American tradition. Smoking or smudging a room or a house is a way of purifying it, of chasing away undesirable energy and memories, and of blessing a space. This is a powerful healing technique.

Take dried sage or cedar leaves and burn them in an incense burner or on some igniting charcoal in a bowl or dish. Walk slowly around the room, allowing the smoke to lift, waft, and fill the corners and edges of the space. Pay special attention to areas of the house where your ex spent the most time: the TV area, the couch, the other side of the bed. Smudging these areas, along with the windows and doors of the house, somehow makes you feel safer and protected. It really feels as if the house is cleansed and filled with new energy.

5. *Removing the ring ritual.* One of the most difficult moments is when you decide there is no longer a reason to wear your wedding ring. A ring is an ancient symbol of unity and love, and to remove it is a powerful act. It is both physically and emotionally painful, and it sends the message "It's over" to your inner self. Often the ring finger has been dented and reshaped by wearing the wedding ring.

We suggest that you set up for this ritual in the following way: Fill the bathroom sink with warm, scented water. Place hand lotion, soft soap, and fluffy towels near the sink. Have some fresh-cut flowers in a vase nearby and a few candles lit. Play soft music in the background, if you wish.

When you are ready, approach the bathroom sink and being by massaging hand lotion into your fingers and your hands. Look at yourself in the mirror, right into your own eyes, and softly say over and over again, "I am lovable."

Next, immerse your hands in the warm water and work the soap around all of your fingers. As you soften up the ring finger and remove the ring, look into your eyes in the mirror and repeat several times, "I deserve love." This ought to sound like a soft, sincere chant.

Rinse your hands and lovingly dry them. Send your hands a message of love and thanks for all they do for you. Place the ring in a special box, or shell, or other place. Hold your own hand gently and look into the mirror, repeating to yourself, "I love you."

If you begin to cry at any time during this ritual, don't hold back. Let the tears flow because this is a powerful healing ritual and tears are a spiritual release and emotional cleansing. Keep reminding yourself that you are lovable, that you deserve love, and that you are sending love to yourself.

When you finish crying, and at some point you will, gently wash your face and lie down. Relax, take it easy; you have just gone through a big release and you deserve a break.

6. *Replacing the ring ritual*. This ritual is the same as the former, but at some point in the process you can embellish the action by removing the old wedding ring and replacing it with a special new ring bought specifically for this purpose. After wearing a ring for many years, it is reassuring to have something on the same finger. The important aspect of this act is that you love and appreciate yourself by placing this new ring on the wedding ring finger. The ring ought to be very special to you and, ideally, it *doesn't* look at all like a wedding ring.

7. *Life mate ring ceremony*. This ritual is similar to the previous one for replacing the ring, but at some point in the process you can embellish the action by visualizing the new ring as the special wedding ring your life mate will place on your finger. Get a clear picture in your mind of your life mate standing next to you, in a beautiful environment, as he/she takes your hand and places the new ring on your finger. Picture how everything looks

around you, hear all the sounds, feel the emotions and feelings. Touch the ring. Be very aware of its shape, texture, and temperature as you feel it go on your finger. The more intensity you bring to the physical and emotional experience, the more powerful the message will be to your subconscious mind.

Manifestation Rituals

Now you are ready to create dramatic changes in your life. Manifestation rituals are magic, and they work. Be careful what you ask for—you just might get it, depending on your level of skill. The better you get and the more confidence you feel, the more powerful your results will be. That is why we say again—be careful what you ask for.

RITUAL TO CALL TO YOUR IDEAL LIFE MATE

This is a ritual that you must invent for yourself. It ought to reflect your deepest sense of beauty and your inner wishes and dreams. Choose a space that you love, and open the space for the ritual in a way that has meaning for you.

Smudge the space, ask for guidance, and begin to meditate or pray for your ideal life mate to manifest in your life soon.

Emphasize your Five Qualities of Satisfaction.

Chant or sing to him or her; create a dance or a poem.

Give profound thanks for the opportunity to live on this beautiful earth, and to be loving and giving, ready to share your love.

Close the space.

Mary's Ritual

Each time I performed my manifestation ritual I would open the space with some kind of chant, usually spontaneous, but here's an example:

> I consecrate and bless this space for the purpose of healing
> and manifesting forgiveness and love. I ask the blessings of
> the directions—North, East, South, West—and the
> elements—Earth, Air, Fire, Water—the forces of nature, to
> align with me and guide me. I ask for strength and support, for
> love and forgiveness, to authentically pour from within my
> being. Bless this space and all who are in it.

I'd sit down and begin to meditate. Then I would smudge and smoke the loft, waving the yin and yang wands through the smoke, singing something haunting.

I would pull cards from the tarot deck and interpret them, or sing some more, or meditate and pray.

Then I would count my blessings, give deep thanks for all the good in my life, and send energy to all whom I love.

Last I would close the space:

> I now close this space, giving heartfelt thanks for the honor
> of these blessings and this healing ceremony. We thank all
> who joined to assist our forgiveness process, and return this
> space to its former use. Thank you God, Goddess, and All
> that Is.

A Manifestation Chant

This chant is designed to send your magic Five Qualities of Satisfaction out into the universe. It is very effective when done in nature, standing over a waterfall or a stream. Some form of moving water is the best.

Position yourself over the water so that you are close to it but stable enough that you won't fall in. It is great to use a rattle or drum and begin to shake or pound it over the water. Find a nice, emphatic beat and keep the sound going.

Take one of your Five Qualities and begin to chant it to the beat of the rattle. It might be nice to start by chanting, "I deserve the best," just to get into the flow of the chant. Then find a way to chant each of the remaining qualities as you rattle.

Send the energy of the chant out and into the water, and watch the water flow out into the streams, lakes, and oceans of the world. Know that your request is flowing on the water out into the universe. Your ideal life mate will be awakened by the call of this chant as the words are carried on the water. Words have power; water has power; emotional intention and desire have power. For this ritual, you combine all of these powerful tools.

Rattle and chant, letting the emotional energy build to a peak, and then just rattle and rattle. Gradually let the sounds fade away, and sit for a while in the beauty and silence. Hear the sound of your heartbeat, feel the power of the water. Silently give thanks to the water and the Life Force. Thank the space, and close the space when you are ready.

LIFE MATE MANIFESTATION RITUAL

This life mate manifestation ritual is composed of a series of very powerful movements and gestures that allow you to "step into" your Five Qualities of Satisfaction. This is an adaptation of a routine invented by Tim Piering. We have modified it to include the desired qualities for your ideal life mate.

We suggest that you do this exercise every day, at least once. Ideally, this process should take place at sunrise or sunset, or both. The very best time is dawn, before you start your day. This is because first thing in the morning, you are still a little sleepy, and in a vulnerable open state of awareness. The right side of your brain is still active, having been in the dream state all night long. The left side, or more logical, rational side of your personality, is still trying to wake up. This is a very good time to meditate, to write in your journal, and to do this exercise because your mind is open to suggestion.

1. Start by standing with your feet planted flat, toes facing forward, feet about shoulder's width apart, knees slightly bent, and your hands resting together in front of you.

2. Bring your hands up above your shoulders, in front and outstretched and touching one another. Your two thumbs are touching and your first fingers are touching at the tips, forming a rounded triangle. Focus your attention and look up through the space between your fingers. Imagine the entire universe framed there. Imagine the power of the universe, and slowly bring your hands down to your sides, making a fist with your right hand and keeping your left hand open and flat. Slam the side of your right fist into the flat of your left hand, ending in a quick punch at the bottom. This movement relates to the gathering of Ki (or Life Force energy) in the martial arts. With this movement you pull the power of the universe in to yourself.

3. Imagine a time when you were in love, when you felt the strong passion and emotions of a beautiful love. Remember the feeling, not the person they were attached to. Build up the feeling, and when you have it, see yourself standing in front of you, filled with that love. See yourself as a shining, beautiful, smiling creature, filled with light and spirit.

This is you at your best, the most powerful and beautiful manifestation of you, filled with radiant love. When you have a strong clear picture, step into that *you*.

4. Step right into the space, feel the emotions wash over your body as you become that radiant being, the strong and loving individual you really are. Breathe deep and let those feelings fill you with joy. And from this space, send energy to your life mate, somewhere across time and space. Send the energy of love and light to that person, know that he or she will receive it on his or her end of the web of life.

5. Step into each of your qualities in invisible boxes on the ground:

First Box. See a box on the ground in front of you, one step up and to the far left. Put the first magic Quality of Satisfaction in that box. Maybe the quality is "sense of humor." Step into that box and let that quality fill you and energize you. Feel your own sense of humor send out the feeling to your life mate.

Second box. Step to your right into the box that is your second magic Quality of Satisfaction. Perhaps it is "great sexual connection." Really let that feeling flood your being. Feel your own sexuality blossom and expand. Send those feelings out into the universe to your life mate.

Third to fifth boxes. Now step to the right again into your third quality, then the fourth, then the fifth. Go through each magic Quality of Satisfaction and really let yourself experience the feelings in each. Send those feelings out from each box to your ideal life mate and know that that person receives it telepathically, through the connection of the powerful web of life.

6. Now step once more forward and ahead into a box of profound spiritual feelings of gratitude, the Blessing Box. Thank God or the Goddess, or the Universal Life Force. Give thanks for your life, your health, your ability to love and laugh, to dream and vision. Bless your life mate and send a message of love to that person.

7. Step backward several steps, and gather the energy and power of each of the boxes you had stepped into. Gather and pull the energy and love back into your own body, then hold it as the treasure that it is. Give yourself a hug, and step out into your day filled with feelings of love and power.

INNER MARRIAGE CEREMONY

Plan your wedding! Through this ritual you will have the opportunity to experience one of the most powerful of all human rituals: the Wedding Ceremony.

Write your ceremony in advance so you will have the words available. Imagine that an official will be performing the ceremony, or ask a friend to play the role of minister, priest, or other official to help you really experience this ritual. Memorize your ceremony script, learn your lines.

Create a beautiful space in nature, or use an indoor space as your "chapel." Decorate an altar, place vases of flowers everywhere, define an aisle to walk up, and so on. Get dressed up, play the wedding march music, and make your grand entrance walking down the aisle.

Go through the actions of the wedding ceremony as a healing ritual for your own heart. You are marrying the inner male and female, you are healing your heart, opening up to the beauty of uniting with your life mate. You are taking a powerful step in making your dreams come true.

Enjoy these powerful rituals and ceremonies, and feel free to create your own personal rituals to bring focus to the events in your own life. Using the steps and guidelines, you can invent rituals to attract your life mate, to increase your career success, to buy a piece of real estate, or anything else you can imagine.

It is the power of your beliefs, the intensity of your physical and emotional energy, the focus of your mind, that bring about the magic in your life.

9.

Guided Meditations and Journeys

The subconscious mind loves fantasy. Going into states of deep trance or deep relaxation to fantasize about love provides the opportunity to contact and guide the subconscious mind to heal itself and to manifest changes in your life. This technique has been used by healers and shamans for centuries, and is used in therapy today.

Give the mind positive tasks to do and it will do them. If you don't set constructive tasks for your mind to do, it will randomly search for something to think about.

The mind tends to attach itself to negative concepts if they are presented. If positive thoughts are introduced, the mind will just as easily switch to those. In computer jargon, this is called GIGO, for "Garbage In, Garbage Out." Because the mind will grab on to whatever is provided, be sure to provide loving information, such as compliments, visualizations, positive thoughts, and acknowledgments as often as possible.

The guided journeys we have shared in this chapter will provide your mind with positive loving images. They are designed to be recorded and listened to over and over, because repetition is the way the mind learns new concepts.

Use these three guided meditations to facilitate your inner journey toward healing your past loves, forgiving yourself and others, and attracting your ideal life mate. We use these in our workshops, and the participants love them. They are powerful meditations.

We suggest that you read these meditation journeys out loud and tape record yourself. Play soft music in the background. You will be listening to them over and over again.

The first meditation takes you into your inner garden, where you will be able to heal yourself and others, and you can speak to your past lovers as well as your future ideal life mate. You will be able to receive guidance and acknowledgment, relaxation and peace, happiness and feelings of love.

JOURNEY 1

This garden meditation is a deeply acknowledging and loving tour of your inner garden. Your garden is a place to heal yourself and others, to ask for and receive guidance, to learn self-acceptance and self-love. The garden is your own special place, an inner sanctuary and retreat from the physical world. It is where you communicate with your higher self and your subconscious mind. The garden is a place of discovery and pure love.

(Begin the music, start the tape, and begin reading slowly and softly.)

Garden Meditation

Come with us now on a special journey—an adventure into the magical land of your own deepest inner self, to a special garden, a place that is beautiful, that is peaceful, that is deeply healing and totally joyful. Your inner garden is always there, a place you can always go to learn, to rest, to nourish yourself, to ask for guidance. Let's go there now.

Start by taking a few deep breaths. Breathe deeply in and

out, in and out. Slowly breathing in ... and out ... breathing in ... and on each exhale breathing out all tension ... and totally relaxing ... really let yourself go—that's right. Try breathing in through the crown of your head ... and out through your navel ... again, in through the crown of your head ... and out through your navel. Good. Keep it up as you really relax and let go. This is your special time ... plenty of time ... time to just relax and just be.

As you continue to breathe deeper and deeper, begin to be aware of a path that you are walking on. The path is leading you through a beautiful countryside, and you begin to notice that you are approaching a gate or entryway, just up ahead. As you arrive at this entry, focus your attention on the gate area. Look around and see clearly the colors, the shapes, the outline, any trees and flowers that may be there. Feel the sunshine; feel the breeze passing over your skin. Smell the fragrance in the air and listen for any sounds you may hear. Focus your gaze on one thing now, here at the entryway. See it clearly ... focus on it ... and as you see it more clearly, the gateway opens and you walk inside, into your beautiful garden.

As you enter this special magical place, you feel your senses quicken and your heart leap for joy. This is a garden more beautiful than you've ever seen before. And you know this place; you recognize it. You've been here before. You feel alive here and truly safe. It is a familiar place, one you have visited many many times in your dreams.

As you look around at the gorgeous flowers and trees and the rolling hillsides, the colors and sounds inspire and excite you, and you are moved by the beauty and melody of this place. Take a moment or two and explore your special garden ... look around ... walk around ... run between the hills.

Are there streams or ponds or lakes? Maybe a waterfall nearby? Are there rare flowers or trees, sculptures or works of art? Are there animals or magical creatures living here?

Maybe your power animals visit you in this place. If so, visit them now; see what they have to say to you. Enjoy this special place—your private retreat, your magical garden.

In your exploration of the garden, you gradually find yourself at a very beautiful spot—a place where you feel peaceful, relaxed, centered, and at home ... where you can sit down, breathe, release, and relax. Maybe it's beside a stream or near an ocean, or lake, or waterfall. Take a moment now and make yourself comfortable in this relaxation spot. Sit down and enjoy as you begin to relax and allow yourself to think of all the good things in your life.

Life is wonderful! There are so many things to be thankful for ... so much love ... so much joy. We are so lucky to be alive, to be living in this beautiful human body ... to be living in this magical place ... at this time in history.

Let yourself enjoy thoughts of all the blessings in your life. You are rich in many ways. Think of all the skills you have, the talents you were born with and those you developed. Think of the things you've learned along the path of life, the education you've had along the journey, the people you've met, the friends you've made, all the things you've learned, the way you've grown. You have turned out so well!

Remember the good times you've shared with friends who love you—family members who care about you so deeply, times you've shared with lovers, with loved ones. And the good times you've spent alone ... with yourself.

There are so many people who love you, who appreciate you. Let their faces appear as you think about how much they love you, how much you love them. You are loved and appreciated by many many people—friends, co-workers, family. These people love you very very much and are so grateful you are alive and that you are in their lives. They are so thankful to be your friend. Spend a moment with them ... thank them and send your love.

You are loved ... you are appreciated ... you have turned out so well. And as you listen to the voices, allow these words to go deeper and fill your inner well of love. Imagine that these messages come from all of your friends and family . . . your loved ones . . . and from your own higher self:

> You are loved and you are blessed. We love you . . . We love you . . . We appreciate you . . . You are so special . . . We support you. You are blessed . . . We are on your team . . . We want the best for you—in your career, in your family life, in your personal life, in your love life, in your relationships . . . All the best. We want you to win. You are a total success . . . you have turned out so well. Everything is working out perfectly. We appreciate you . . . you bring such joy to our lives. You are lightness and happiness. We love you . . . you are a child of God . . . a child of the Goddess . . . the Universal Life Force and all that is . . . you are love . . . and joy . . . and sheer energy and light. . . .
>
> The world is a mysterious and beautiful place, full of magic and surprises. You are a light being . . . a pure spirit of joy and adventure. You are here to enjoy life! . . . to have pleasure and joy and love. This universe is a garden of delights. An "E ticket" ride of incredible happiness and excitement . . . This is your playground, your vacation, your paradise. Enjoy your life! It is a gift and a blessing. You are blessed! You are loved! We love you. We love you. We love you.

And as you let these feelings fill your inner well, restoring, healing, renewing, and refreshing you, just let yourself overflow with love . . . and peace . . . and joy—enough for you and enough for everyone who comes into your life . . . As you feel yourself flowing with heartfelt love and beauty, as you realize throughout your entire being that you are loved and you are blessed, you begin to feel the presence of another being. Someone has joined you here in this beautiful spot . . . someone you love, respect, and honor . . . one who is the source of wisdom and love in your life.

As you greet this being, take a moment to ask for guidance

or advice. Ask a question, and know that your inner self knows exactly what to ask for, what it wants and needs ... and it is asking right now. Listen to the advice ... perhaps it is a message ... or a smile ... or a gift of some kind. Receive this gift, reflect on its meaning ... and give thanks. This gift is a blessing and a symbol of love and wisdom. This is a gift for you to take with you. Now thank this being for the guidance and prepare to walk back through your beautiful garden ... back past the flowers and the trees, past the waterfall and streams. ...

On your way to the gateway, you come to a beautiful, majestic fountain. This gorgeous fountain is the fountain of life ... of energy and prosperity, health, Life Force. Power, beauty, and happiness all flow in rainbow showers from this beautiful fountain. Joyfully walk to the magnificent fountain and cup the shimmering water in your hands. Drink from the fountain of happiness, prosperity, health, beauty, and love. Splash the water on your face and body, and as you do you receive a power blessing from the fountain itself:

> From this moment on, you are blessed with the very essence of life. You are loved by all people and things. You are loved and you are love. You will always receive the best that life has to offer. Run your hands over every part of your body now, filling it with white light and love. This blessing will last the rest of your life. You will always expect the best and always receive the best: inner peace, joy, happiness, health, prosperity, and love. You are loved and you are blessed. Relate to all people you meet with love from this moment on, and you will receive love from all people. Now let this feeling flow through your entire body and know that you are loved and you deserve the best. Starting now, you will always receive the best that life has to offer. You are blessed!

With love, light, and beauty filling your heart, you thank the fountain and continue to walk through the garden toward the gateway. You are overflowing with love, joy, mana, Life Force, and happiness. As you approach the gateway, recognize the flowers and trees that grow there, the colors and shapes.

And now, leaving the garden, you turn to look back, smiling with joy and happiness, for you know that this garden is here for you whenever you need or want to visit it. This is your special place, a private sanctuary, always waiting inside to fill you with love and strength.

And as your attention comes back to the physical plane now, you become aware of your body again. You are filled with love and joy, and the knowledge that you are truly loved and blessed. And as you become fully aware, stretching and moving your body, opening your eyes, know that you are a blessing and we love you . . . we love you . . . we love you.

That is the end of the garden meditation. It is a very loving and relaxing experience, and we sincerely hope that you took advantage of the opportunity to tape-record the entire script for yourself with soft, beautiful music in the background. We have created a professional version of this meditation tape that can be ordered using the address in Appendix C of this book.

Our clients have found that this meditation works very well for healing past loves and painful issues or memories. You can insert any particular issue you want to heal, bring that issue or painful memory with you into the garden, ask for advice or input from your guides, and really listen to the messages you receive.

JOURNEY 2

This guided journey meditation was created to help a very dear friend release herself from her past relationships and forgive all the men in her past. This ritual of the cave asserts the power of femininity as it frees, releases, and forgives the loves of the past.

The meditation was performed in a huge dry cave on the island of Kauai, but it can be in any cavelike environment—a forest grove, a protected rock overhang, or even a closet or darkened room.

The cave is a metaphor for femininity, for the inner nature of women's sexuality, the receptivity and surrender, the dark, safe, enclosed opening. The cave is the womb, the mother, the warm, safe space within. This will help to heal any issues that you may have had with your mother or father in the past.

Start this journey by tape-recording the meditation. You can use your own voice with some soft music in the background. Read the words slowly and clearly. Breathe deeply as you read aloud into the tape; take your time and let your voice become soft and soothing.

Once you have recorded the tape, or have ordered our professional version of it, you can take this journey over and over again.

When you play the tape, breathe deeply and relax. Begin to think of the ways you are loved and blessed in your life.

(Begin the music, start the tape, and begin reading slowly and softly.)

The Cave of Forgiveness

Begin by breathing in warmth and light and love ... and breathing out any tension in your body. Let your eyes gently close. Breathe in light, and breathe out tension. Relax, meditate, and reflect on how blessed you are in your life. Breathe in and out, and begin to see a vision of yourself walking along the ocean. You are walking down a white sandy beach, the waves are lapping at your feet, and the water is a light turquoise blue.

As you walk, you begin to see a huge mountain up ahead; it's as though the beach runs alongside a huge cliff face, and as you search the side of the mountain, you see the entrance to a cave, almost covered with jungle vines. You walk toward the cave and see a small waterfall alongside the face of the mountain. You step through the waterfall and pull the vines to the side so that you can see the entrance to the cave more clearly.

As your eyes adjust to the darkness, you see that there is a huge dry cavern inside, and with excitement and curiosity you step inside the cave. Immediately, it is cool and dry, and you feel very, very safe in here. You explore the cave and find wondrous rock formations and maybe even some cave paintings on the walls. You come to a circle of rocks that looks like a gathering place, and you sit on the largest and flattest rock.

You feel very comfortable, and sigh with relief as you let the strength of the rock support you. Your eyes are closed, and you begin to relax and drift in the quiet safety of the cave.

As you breathe in and out, you gradually become aware of a line of people approaching you. You see and hear and feel the presence, the sights and sounds of people whom you begin to recognize. As you see familiar faces you come to the awareness that this line of people is made up of those you have loved in the past.

Wives, husbands, lovers, all pass before you now. They are filled with love and light, and as they pass you feel the love radiating off each one of them.

Like a beautiful parade of lovers, they pass before your consciousness now, smiling and strong, sending the love they felt your way. As each one moves past, remember the love you felt . . . remember the love they gave.

Thank each one for the lessons you learned. Whether they were pleasant or painful, they were important lessons for you at that time in your life.

Thank them one at a time for assisting your growth and evolution, bless them on their own journey, and let them go as they pass by.... The past is past ... there is only the moment. Release them now to go on with your own life. Now see the parade of lovers and let yourself thank, bless, and release each in his or her turn.

Whoever comes to mind is the perfect one. Thank, bless, and release each one....

Now that you have blessed and released all those you've loved, there is one more who loves you very much. He is walking much slower than the others; he seems to carry the weight of a lifetime with him.

Let yourself bring forth a picture of your father now, in the way you love him the most. See him shining in all his power and glory ... feel the warmth and love that he has given you. Know that he has given you all the love that he possibly can; if he had had more to give you, he would have.

We are each only able to give in the ways that we can ... and we each do the best we can. Your father loved you the best way he knew how to ... then ... and now. He loves you in the way he is able to give love ... he receives your love in the way he is able to receive. Let that be enough ... let that be enough. Thank your father for loving you ... thank yourself for loving him ... bless him ... and release him. Forgive him now for all the ways he may have hurt you ... and know that he was unconscious ... that he never wanted to hurt you ... that he has always loved you to the best of his ability. So forgive him now....

Say to yourself, "I forgive you, Dad," and let yourself feel how that feels.

Good. Now let yourself release your father and see him filled with love for you. Send him a bubble of love and let him drift from your consciousness as you become aware of yet another person, walking slowly and softly.

As she comes into view, you realize that this stately, gentle person is your mother. She moves with a grace that comes of life's trials and challenges. She looks up at you and smiles with such warmth and love that you feel you have been kissed by an angel. You smile back and feel the genuine love and warmth that your mother has always given you, in the best ways she knew how.

You smile at her, and thank her for all the things she gave you, all the lessons you learned. Send her love and gratitude, appreciation and happiness. Say out loud to yourself, "I love you Mother, I forgive you."

She gives a little wave and follows the others out of the cave, leaving trails of shimmering love behind them.

You are now aware that you have always given the love you have ... that you have been generous with your love ... and that you are capable of giving and receiving love that is beautiful and healthy and pure. Know in your heart of hearts that you deserve love ... that you are a good and deserving person with the best of intentions, that you are lovable. And know that there are many who love you, who send you their love and warmth right now, all of your family and friends, all of your angels and guides, all of your lovers.

As you begin to come back to the surface now, remember that you are loved. Feel the movement of the wind against your skin ... feel the temperature around you ... feel your hands and fingers, your legs, feet, and toes. Begin to stretch and return to this time and place as you come fully awake, refreshed, and renewed.

JOURNEY 3

This is a special journey we have designed for calling to your ideal life mate. It activates the threads in the web of life and sends a message of love and longing and readiness. This meditation affirms that you know you deserve a love more beautiful than you've ever known before.

There is something very powerful about using your own

voice as the primary sound on the tape. It takes you to an even deeper level of comfort and vulnerability. You may also enjoy playing love songs in the background, since this meditation is designed to connect you with your perfect life mate and partner. We made a tape of "I Am Calling You," alternating the woman's voice with the man's singing the same song. It can be found on the *Baghdad Cafe* movie soundtrack. The music is haunting and effective for this meditation.

Even if you do not tape-record this journey, please *do* read it out loud. It seems to be much more effective when read and heard simultaneously.

Here, now, is the life-mate meditation. Enjoy this beautiful journey. Sit or lie down in a comfortable position and relax as much as you can. The more you relax, the deeper this information can be integrated into your inner self.

(Begin the music, start the tape, and begin reading slowly and softly.)

Journey to the Love Planet

Today is a special day ... this is a beautiful day. Today is the day you will be able to send out a call to your life mate ... to visit and connect with the soul that is your perfect partner. As you relax and go within, know that somewhere in time ... somewhere in space ... there is a person who is looking for you, too.

Relax now and let yourself smile at the thought of your perfect soul mate. Close your eyes ... breathe deep. As you breathe deeply in and out ... in and out ... let your attention focus very gently on the feelings of love you have in your innermost heart—the feelings of warmth and peace that you long to share. Feel the love that fills and overflows your deep inner self. You have so much love to give ... so much to share. You are loved by so many people, appreciated by your families and friends. Now you send this love out into the universe to charge the electrical fields that connect you to your perfect life mate somewhere across time and space.

And as you continue to breathe in and out slowly, let yourself go even deeper. Really relax and let go so that you can gain maximum benefit from this journey. Let yourself go, drift and dream. Float and dance on the clouds, feel yourself getting lighter and lighter—so light that you seem to drift up into the sky. Gently, softly, you begin to realize that you are floating. Gliding, flying, soaring, gracefully, through clouds and sunlight, through rainbows and misty mornings. Flying and gliding across mountains, and valleys, oceans, beaches, and coastal areas, over lakes and streams. Follow a stream until it becomes a beautiful waterfall, dive and cascade over the cliffs, becoming part of the waterfall, laughing and dancing with the water itself, playing in the magical wonders of water, and light, and wind.

Now let yourself glide again up into the sky, way way up into the sunset, into the twilight sky as the sun sinks and the night's velvety drapes surround you and the sparkling stars peek out into the clear, dark void. Fly now toward a very bright star . . . the brightest star in the night sky, a twinkling light that seems to call your name. It pulls you and sings to you with a voice of silvery love. Laughter and happiness sparkle from this beautiful star, which grows bigger and brighter as you get closer and closer.

The star is definitely calling to you now: "Come home . . . come home to me . . . you are welcome here . . . you are loved . . . I've been waiting for you, waiting so long.

And as you move closer you see that this large star is a planet . . . Venus, the love planet . . . a glowing, gorgeous planet that hums with happiness and life. Gradually you are drawn to one spot on the planet that seems to be especially beautiful, and you decide to land there. Flying gently down to your love planet now, you come to a perfect landing, laughing with delight at the sheer fun of the ride. Look around . . . enjoy the view . . . this is your own special place and an entire planet of love that you have created. This place is magical and yet at the same time it is comfortable, filling you with feelings of safety and love and comfort. You are safe here . . . you are loved here . . . you can relax . . . you are home.

The love planet is haunting and mystical . . . magical and awe-inspiring. You look around and discover many beautiful things. All of your favorite things are here . . . your favorite foods grow on trees . . . your favorite colors fly like flags . . . and as you walk amongst the many wonders, you find that you have come to a tree that has a stairway along its huge trunk. They look like steps going up the sides of the trunk. You look up into the branches far above, and see a wonderful tree house . . . a play house . . . a dream house. You are eager to climb up the stairs to the tree house, and as you go to take the first step, you see that there are words written on the step.

It says, "You Are Loved . . . You Are Blessed." The words are engraved into the step. And as you take the first step you smile, knowing that you're re-stepping into the state of knowing deep in your inner heart that you are truly loved and magnificently blessed . . . that you are a loving person yourself who has so much to give . . . and wants so much to receive.

As you step up to take the next step on the tree, you see that it is inscribed with the words, "You Deserve the Best" and you think to yourself how true this statement is. As you take the step you feel how deeply you deserve the best in life and in love. Perhaps in the past you have settled for situations and relationships that were not the best . . . but you learned and grew from these experiences, receiving great knowledge and lessons . . . and now you know with every cell in your body that you *do* deserve the best because you are willing to give the best.

You are filled with joy as you step up into the state of knowing that you deserve the best that life has to offer you . . . the best love . . . the most beautiful life mate . . . a partner who will love you and treat you with the utmost respect and who will honor the love the two of you share.

As you go to take the next few steps, you see that the step is marked with the word "Confidence." You realize that you now have the confidence it takes to commit yourself and your love to another human being. That your confidence will support you, and that your ideal life mate does exist and is looking for you at this very moment. Feel how much you will appreciate the quality of confidence when you see it manifested in your life mate.

And now pull yourself up and climb to the next step. Read the inscription on this step as you ease yourself up. It says, "The Joy of Giving and Happiness of Receiving." Smile as you rest on this step for a moment, filling yourself with the joy of giving. How much fun it is to give to those you love! How delightful to receive their gifts!

Let the awareness dawn that in order to give you must allow yourself to receive . . . that giving and receiving are connected creating a golden ring, each completing the circle of abundance and love. Fill yourself with the knowledge that you can give and receive fully, and that there is a person who is longing to give you exactly these qualities . . . and much much more.

The next step glows with a magical light, and as you climb up to read it you feel a profound connection with your higher self. The inscription reads, "Spiritual Connection with Your Source" and tears of joy run down your cheeks as you realize that your life mate will try to understand you at the very source of your being . . . and that you will cherish the connection between your higher selves. There is nothing as beautiful as the spiritual contact that life mates share. The deepest inner strengths and secrets are revealed . . . the sheer white light of consciousness and life force connection is completed. It is as high as two humans can go together . . . the ultimate state of love.

Let this fifth step fill you with its power, and know that by stepping into each of these qualities you have activated them fully in your subconscious mind. Right this minute they are working to attract your life mate to you.

Pull yourself up to the next level, which simply says "Appreciation" and gratefully acknowledge how much you appreciate the many gifts of this lifetime. Thank God, the Goddess, and all that is for the supreme gift of life ... and send thanks and appreciation to all the people you love—people who have helped you to grow ... people who have loved you.

And step up one more step, which simply reads "Congratulations." Smile as you celebrate your ability to affirm that you deserve all the things you have asked for because you are a good and loving person. Celebrate your ability to ask for what you want ... celebrate the self-esteem it takes to know you deserve it.

And now you see one final step ahead of you. It reads, "Step Forward into Love, Pleasure, and Ecstasy." And as you take the final step you are filled with such incredible feelings of bliss and joy. As you step into your tree house a shower of electricity and soft-colored light cascades over you, filling you with radiant energy and star sparkles. You shimmer and shine ... like a star. The starlight shines from you casting a glow over the interior of the tree house as you radiate light and love.

And your heart leaps as you see a figure across the room ... a dimly lit figure who radiates the same light ... and you begin to see thin bands of light connecting you to each other across time and space ... across the room. You both stand still as the night sky swirls outside and the moon passes by. You are locked in each other's gaze as the night sky gradually changes to dawn and the sunshine streams in the many windows and the sun passes by. You and your life mate stand across the universe ... so close and yet so far ... and slowly you move toward each other ... like vast spinning planets ... like stars across distant galaxies ... like the sun and the moon ... linked by love and gravity ... held in the essential tension of time, space, mass, and light ... circling the earth forever out of reach, forever gazing on the shadows of each other's beauty. You feel the pull of the intense burning love ... the wash of the sea and tides.

Gradually step closer to the figure across from you. Feel the pull of exquisite tension . . . the longing. Speak words of love to each other . . . tell of your longing and your search . . . lay bare your soul and vow to love each other . . . to give unendingly . . . to cherish the gift of each other's love . . . and like the sun and moon, which can never meet *but do* in the rare and passionate eclipse. Run to each other across the room . . . across time-space reality. Hold each other, hugging and kissing in a tangle of passion and union that must be fulfilled. Feel the joy overflow from your bodies as you laugh and play . . . talk and kiss . . . make love and hold each other and know that telepathically, far down on planet earth, your life mate has picked up the love in both realities . . . in many realities . . . and that all walls have evaporated between you.

Send out the love to your life mate somewhere across time and space . . . and know that the message is received . . . as you continue to dance and laugh and love . . . until the eclipse has fused you into the divine union of two souls who love with the connection of universal source. Then drift and dream the dream of your combined lives . . . the freedom of the dream of joy and friendship, love and spiritual union. Dance the dance together . . . dream the dream . . . and know that your love fuels the universe . . . that love is the power that sustains the dream . . . that your love gives energy and light to the whole of creation . . . that you are filling the storehouses of love all across the universe . . . that others benefit from your love . . . that you heal the pains and ills of the world with your love . . . as you love and love and love.

And now, with the dawn of another day that never ends, you wake yourself. You move away from each other in the treehouse, smiling and joyful in the strength of your individuality . . . the beauty of union heightened by the beauty of separation . . . and you notice that there are many new threads of light connecting you . . . that the threads shimmer with rainbow colors and sparkles . . . and as you drift out the door you send such love to your life mate that reassures both of you of your eminent meetings to come.

You will see each other again, and very soon . . . and you will be able to return to the love planet to be together any time that you choose to. So with love and deep gratitude, you let yourself drift out the treehouse window . . . out into the night sky . . . past the moon and the dawning sunlight . . . out into the universe . . . until you find yourself back in this time and space reality . . . back in this beautiful human body on this magical planet earth . . . and you move and shift in your body to wake it up, stretching the luxurious stretch of deep relaxation . . . and come back into the room and full awareness. Take a deep breath. Welcome back.

Use these meditation tapes often, ideally every night before falling asleep. These inner journeys provide positive loving affirmations and subtle suggestions for your subconscious mind to put into action.

Repetition is the fastest way for the brain to learn new information. The more you use the tools provided in this chapter, as well as the entire book, the more the brain will learn and the faster the changes in your life will take place.

10.

Walk with Me
My Love, and Hold
My Hand and Dream

We are including this final chapter because we feel so positive that if you have been doing the program outlined in this book, you have attracted several possible ideal life mates by now.

So first of all we want to say, "Congratulations on having attracted your ideal life mate!" And if you haven't yet, congratulations on being willing to read this section to prepare yourself to set up a partnership that works for you.

You deserve a relationship that is intimate, trusting, and spiritual as well as successful. Let's be sure that you are setting yourself up for success this time.

How can you be sure that the relationship you have attracted is really "the one"? The way you test to be sure is to go back through your Five Qualities of Satisfaction and be *sure* that this person really does fulfill the criteria for your ideal life mate. Don't cheat just because you feel very strongly about the person. Be honest and clear-headed, and look closely to see if the qualities are met.

Maybe you discover that he or she fulfills only three out of your five criteria. What should you do?

At this point, you must decide if you really do want and deserve the kind of love you *say* you want. You can settle for three out of five, because the person is wonderful and has many other wonderful qualities.

Or you can choose to date this person and enjoy the companionship and love, knowing that this person is not "the one." Be honest with yourself and with the other person; tell the individual that you don't really see this relationship becoming serious, but that you enjoy his or her company and don't mind seeing him or her occasionally.

Or you can be firm with yourself, knowing that if you do not create standards for yourself, no one else will. It takes a lot of courage to be alone rather than with someone who is "almost right." But if you don't, you will never know if the ideal life mate—the one with all Five Qualities of Satisfaction—was waiting for you around the next corner on your life journey.

Take the time to check carefully your Five Qualities of Satisfaction and determine how many of these characteristics your new love has.

HOW DO YOU KNOW THAT YOU ARE READY?

There is an old saying that goes, "When the student is ready, the teacher will appear." We amend that to, "When you are ready, your life mate will appear." It will probably happen when you least expect it, when you are feeling very balanced and have a lot of self-esteem and feelings of self-love. When you are no longer needy, when you are not looking, when you are simply going about the business of your own happy, fulfilled life, the ideal person will show up. There are countless stories of this truth. Ask anyone who is in an ideal relationship or in a happy marriage, and he or she will probably say, "I wasn't really looking for a relationship" and go on to tell you the story of how they met.

If you are not ready, keep working on yourself. Read the first half of this book again and *do all the exercises* this time!

If you are not ready, you will be attracting people who are not right for you, but you will be able to spot that, using your five qualities as a guide. If you are not ready, enjoy your life at whatever stage it is in. Remember, you deserve the best! That includes the best experience of being single.

COULD YOU HAVE ALREADY FOUND HIM OR HER AND NOT REALIZED IT?

You may be able to transform a current relationship into your life-mate relationship. You may have had bliss sitting right under your nose and not realized it.

Take a good look at your Five Qualities of Satisfaction. See if the person you have been seeing might be "the one" all along! Although the chances of this happening seem pretty slim to us, it is possible that you already have someone wonderful in your life whom you are taking for granted.

THE WINDOW OF OPPORTUNITY

Once you have found your ideal life mate—you are sure it is the right person and you are falling head over heels in love—be aware of your window of opportunity. This is a very powerful window in time, and how you handle it can make or break the relationship.

On the one hand, you must seize the moment: take action to help and encourage the relationship to begin. On the other hand, you must use extreme caution to listen to the inner direction that will guide you to the highest and best good for you. Either way, you must be willing to make changes.

When you meet your ideal life mate, your life will change dramatically. You may change houses, states, countries; you may change jobs or friends; and you may change the way you spend your time. Literally everything can and probably will change about your life.

Many people are not ready for such a radical change, and they resist the love relationship because it poses such a huge threat to their sense of self. Especially as people get older and perhaps more set in their ways, enormous changes can be upsetting. This is one major reason why some people *never* attract their ideal life mate. They do not want to go through the life changes that come with a new relationship.

Be prepared for change. As you are working on yourself, let your mind and Higher Self know that you want a change, that you are ready for a change, that you embrace the changes that lie ahead.

TRUSTING YOUR HEART—THE INNER VOICE

There is a deep inner voice in each of our hearts that knows what to do in every situation. But this voice is not to be confused with the chattering voice of the inner editor, critic, or self-destroyer.

The true inner voice is the voice of the heart, or perhaps the voice of the Higher Self. It is a soft, calm, peaceful voice that can give tremendous guidance when we listen to it.

When you meet your life mate, you will know. The inner voice will sing to you, will call to you in your dreams.

When Mary met Don, she experienced a deep sense of inner peace. Her inner voice said quietly but firmly, "This is it, you are safe, you are home, you can relax now." For Don, the inner voice was saying, "Let's be together." His motivation was more of a feeling, an inner knowing that "everything felt right."

Many couples we know have shared similar feelings upon meeting each other. They "just knew" that this was the right person.

Tune into your inner voice. Listen to it. Is it saying, "This is it. This is the one!" Or is it saying, "I don't know about this...." Listen to that inner voice, and use the road map of your Five Qualities of Satisfaction.

Helen, a woman in her forties, had met a man she liked very much. He wasn't really the kind of man she had previously considered to be "her type," but she felt powerfully drawn to him.

One night she came home after being out on a date with him. He kissed her good-night at her door, and she went inside. As she shut the door and turned toward the living room of her house, she heard an inner voice so loud she almost jumped. The voice said, "That is the man you will marry."

She was so stunned she looked around the room to see if someone was there. Then she realized it was a voice inside her own head.

As things turned out, two years later she did marry that man. Although he was not her "type," he had all of her Five Qualities of Satisfaction. He had the inner qualities that mattered to her, and her inner voice recognized those qualities even before her conscious mind had seen them.

That is why we recommend keeping an open mind. Don't judge too hastily. Listen to your inner voice and thoroughly check to see whether you have attracted your ideal life mate, but not yet recognized the person!

NEW PERSON, NEW EXPERIENCE

It is extremely important to start the life-mate relationship with a new mind, a young heart, and a fresh outlook. It is tempting to make assumptions about the new relationship based on experiences and learnings from old relationships. But resist all tendencies to make assumptions about your new love. This is not the same person from your past and you are not the same person you were, either. You have worked long and hard to change and evolve; now it is time to put the new learning into practice.

Do not be harsh or critical with each other. Don't judge. See what is positive and good about your partner and emphasize what works. Emphasize the love and it will flourish.

For example, early in their life-mate relationship, Mary realized that whenever she predicted Don's behavior and made assumptions about his actions, *she was wrong*. She invented a new mantra: "New person, new experience . . ." and chanted it whenever necessary.

Don was so much more sensitive and caring than any man she had ever known before that she found herself misjudging him whenever she compared the old with the new. Don simply did things differently (thank God), and therefore she was inspired to do things differently also.

Everything is different about your new partner. First and foremost, you are life mates so there is an entirely different spiritual quality and sense of purpose to the relationship. The sexuality is totally different, the chemistry is different, the levels of caring and thoughtfulness are different.

Be gentle with your new love. Let the union be the source of your joy and strength together. Be caring and thoughtful in your interactions with each other. Place the relationship at the center of your source and every other aspect of your lives will be enhanced.

COMMITMENT

Be willing to commit your love and yourself to your ideal life mate. If you really feel that this person is the one, that he or she fits the qualities you are looking for and you feel love and happiness when you are together, then seize the moment and commit to each other.

A beautiful romantic partner is a rare miracle. If you have found each other, then go ahead and commit to each other. To commit is to take your love to a much deeper level. It is to grant each other the respect and completion that come only from the ritual and ceremony of marriage.

Go for it; sweep each other away. After falling into each other's love, make the bold move of commitment and go deeper.

In the seventies and eighties a fear of commitment permeated every relationship. But now we detect a shift away from that fear. In the workshops we lead, people are willing and ready to commit to a loving partnership. They have been single long enough to realize that it is not what they want. They bring a new sense of willingness to give and receive love openly.

Don

. . . .

If you feel as though this is the wonderful relationship the likes of which you have only dreamed, really go for it and give it the full commitment.

Don't be afraid to play full out, 100 percent. It's so much more rewarding than holding back and taking a wait-and-see attitude. That can last years and never be fulfilling because neither of you really makes the commitment.

You receive all the rewards when you play 100 percent, so if you feel this is the one, give it your full focus and full attention.

Plan great surprises, commit to it, really enjoy it, and you reap all the rewards.

Mary

. . . .

I would have married Don the first day we got together, that's how sure I was that he was the one I had been searching for. We were really meant for each other, and it was so clear to both of us. He actually proposed after we had been together for about three months, and I was ecstatic.

SWEEP HIM OR HER AWAY

Take the time to discover the small things that make your partner happy. Give the individual things he or she loves, pay attention to details, honor his or her requests. It is very easy to give to each other and it costs nothing. Maybe it's a certain touch or smile, or maybe it's bringing him coffee in bed in the morning. Maybe it's a long massage after a hard day's work or play. Be sensitive and sweet to each other and the relationship will be sheer magic.

Plan ultimate experiences—great surprises, trips, and little gifts and fun things to share. Plan the unusual, the things no one expects. You can really have fun if you give the ultimate, make the stretch.

You can create a dream romance like the kind that exists in fairy tales. It's worth the effort; it's magic.

Don

· ·

When Mary and I first met I was looking forward to the relationship's growing and blossoming into a wonderful friendship and possibly the love of my life. I didn't want to get my expectations too high; I just wanted to give 100 percent of myself and see where it went.

I made some plans that included her coming to the magic island of Kauai for nine days. I offered her a ticket; it wasn't really that much money, but the surprise of it, the time and the location—all alone in a secluded beach house, right after Christmas—made it all the more special. It was love at first kiss.

We barely left the house for nine days except to fly around the island in a helicopter. We just experienced each other, and it was a magical encounter that will stay with us for the rest of our lives.

From there it continued on a whirlwind tour of "How good can it get?" We couldn't stand to be apart after that. I flew to Los Angeles and she picked me up in a limo with a bottle of champagne in the back. Then she whisked me to a beautiful beach house in Venice.

We have beautiful memories that we take such joy in recalling. We swept each other away, creating beautiful memories, and we now have a romance made for movies and fairy tales!

ROMANCE

Once you have had the extreme good fortune of finding your life mate, care and romance can keep the relationship vital and alive. We believe that the honeymoon can last a lifetime. All it takes is focus, sensitivity, and romance.

What has happened to romance? For many modern couples, romance is nonexistent. Perhaps they had some romantic feelings on their honeymoon or in the earliest days of courtship. But now they have settled into the rut of dual-career lives; they are busy all the time and don't have the time to stop and connect with each other.

Women seem innately aware of the value of romance and emotional intimacy in a sexual relationship. It is usually the woman's role to foster an atmosphere of love and romance, to create a romantic mood that allows the spontaneity to happen.

Most men are very emotional and potentially romantic, they just may need help getting started. Once men realize that romance will ultimately bring the results that they want, the rest is easy. If you want pleasure, give pleasure. If you want love, give love. If you want a romantic, fulfilling sex life, give it to your partner.

Women and men alike love romance and intimacy. In life-mate couples, the man takes an active part in the creation of the intimacy. Candles, soft music, a romantic dinner together— all set the mood for openness and caring.

Today, both women and men are opening up to emotional vulnerability, romance, and fulfillment. Expressing deep emotions leads to increased connection and intimacy. Both men and women are more aware of the value of emotional availability, taking responsibility for their actions and thoughts, and listening to and connecting with each other.

Make time for romance in your life. Take a look at your priorities and decide where you can make some shifts so that romance occupies a prominent position. Midday siestas or naps can be very romantic and exciting. If you allow your lives to become extremely busy, if you let yourselves view sex and romance as mundane, your relationship will suffer.

Take romantic weekends and vacations together. Go away to a beautiful spot together, or spend all day at home in bed. Give each other the love and attention you deserve. Remember our mantra for romance: If you want more pleasure, give more pleasure.

Here is a gift that we will share with you. We call it our Prescription For Romance. It is just for fun, a suggested guide for creating more romance in your relationships: Light candles; play soft romantic music; give each other flowers and place them in the environment; give each other romantic cards; wear soft comfortable sensual clothing or lingerie; share romantic meals; have your after-dinner drinks or desserts on the couch or in bed. Be generous with your partner sexually, give pleasure, share what you love and appreciate about each other, and make love often.

Why candles? Why lingerie? Why do all of this? Because, very simply, it works. Candles are a source of beautiful soft light. The flicker of the candlelight induces a light trance and allows the active, conscious mind to tune out and relax. The inner editor shuts off as the brain is soothed and pacified. The light is very beautiful and flattering; your partner suddenly looks beautiful and soft and sexy.

Lingerie is another asset to romance. To wear lingerie brings out the goddess in every woman. Soft sensual fabrics, revealingly cut, trimmed with delicate lace and ribbons, make every woman look and feel gorgeous. There are many types of lingerie, ranging from flowing gowns to teensy g-strings, in every color possible. Treat yourself to lingerie, even if you are single right now. Wear it around the house for the sheer pleasure of it.

Men love lingerie. They love the focus it brings to the sensual parts of their partner; they love the way it looks and feels. Wear it under your business suits, wear it around the house, definitely wear it with your life mate. Surprise each other with new lingerie outfits, and enjoy the beauty of the body freshly bathed and perfumed, and framed in satin and chiffon.

Lingerie is for men, too! There are lots of great-looking satin boxer shorts designed to be evocative. Try the bikinis that have a string for the back for an extra surprise. Men's silk pajama pants are flowing and beautiful, and robes and kimonos come in many sensual fabrics.

In Hawaii and Tahiti, men and women alike wear beautiful hand-painted *pareos*, or sarongs. These garments are colorful and sensual, comfortable, and easy to put on and take off. We even got married wearing *pareos*.

Perfume and cologne are wonderful sensual motivaters for romance. Find the scent that is right for you, explore and experiment with each other, and wear the scent that your lover enjoys the most.

Fill the house with flowers and good smells! Fragrance is very romantic. Smell is one of the most powerful sensory triggers in men and women.

Love and romance create deepened levels of intimacy that touch the essential human spirit, create excitement and passion, and call to a source of union and connection.

We wish you a lifetime of that kind of happiness, romance, love, and connection. Finding your ideal life mate is a gift so wondrous and magical it deserves celebration. Enjoy your love. Honor and celebrate your connection as the divine gift that it is.

Remember to always work on yourselves, keep growing and changing and learning, together and separately.

Thousands of people meet and fall in love every single day. If they can have love, so can you. Focus on the relationships and marriages that *are* working rather than those that aren't.

Become part of the solution: create one of the marriages that work! Live your relationship as one that others can use as inspiration.

But most important, *be* you own ideal life mate. Be loving and forgiving to yourself; appreciate and compliment yourself. Bring the highest and best version of you to the world.

You deserve this love.
You have earned it by your very birth right.
You are love.

Come walk in the garden.
Walk with me, my love
And hold my hand.
. . . and dream.

This is not the end.
This is the beginning.
The best is yet to come.

APPENDIX A
Resources for Healing Past Loves

NEURO LINGUISTIC PROGRAMMING (NLP)

This is an excellent psychological technology for changing the way you view incidents from your past. It is based on research into the way the brain stores information, memories, and emotional input.

NLP is a system of reframing and neurologically changing the way you hold memories in your brain. Using hypnosis and other powerful trance-inducing techniques, the hypnotherapist or NLP practitioner can literally assist you in healing past loves by reframing them in your memory banks.

Mary did a lot of work with NLP healing. She found it extremely effective in healing the pain of her divorce. She was attracted to NLP because it promised (and delivered) fast results. Having come out of her divorce feeling lots of pain and failure, she didn't want to become hard-hearted or jaded about love. She read many books on relationships and healing, and was impressed with Louise Hay's techniques for forgiveness. Dr. Hal Stone's voice dialogue work was also very useful to her.

But her real breakthrough came as she began to work with a very gifted NLP practitioner in Los Angeles, Tim Piering. He used brilliant tools and techniques he had gathered from NLP, hypnosis, and other state-of-the-art psychological techniques. Thanks to these methods, and the masterful, loving skill of the practitioner, she was able to heal her heart in about a year and a half. She credits Tim and his work for being able to heal herself enough to attract someone as wonderful as Don into her life.

LOVING RELATIONSHIPS TRAINING (SONDRA RAY)

Sondra Ray has written many books and has a successful workshop that she teaches all over the world. She uses a technique called re-birthing and the power of positive thought.

Re-birthing releases the traumas and deeply buried fears such as the fear produced by the trauma of birth. Re-birthing releases the five major fears that plague most human beings— what Sondra Ray and Leonard Orr call the "Five Biggies": parental disapproval syndrome, specific negative thought structures, unconscious death urge, birth trauma, and other lifetimes.

Loving Relationships Training is based on the healing power of positive thought. Positive thought works to overcome fear because fear is an emotion, and emotions are due to thoughts.

This training is offered all over the United States and around the world. It is very effective for getting in touch with deeply buried fears and releasing pain.

MAKING LOVE WORK (DR. BARBARA DEANGELIS)

Therapist Barbara DeAngelis has helped thousands of people through her television appearances, successful books, and the training she offers every month at her training center, The Personal Growth Center, in Los Angeles. Her "Making Love Work" training is excellent, a real opportunity to get in touch with blocked emotions and release them.

DeAngelis works with many excellent principles; one of the best is what she calls the Five Levels of Feeling: (1) anger, blame, and resentment; (2) hurt, sadness, and disappointment; (3) fear and insecurity; (4) remorse, regret, and responsibility; (5) love, intention, understanding, and forgiveness. By working through these levels of emotions, she feels that stored pain can be released and love can blossom again.

Mary has taken the "Making Love Work" weekend workshop and found it to be very beneficial.

KEN KEYES CONSCIOUS RELATIONSHIPS

Ken Keyes is a workshop leader and the author of many fine books, including *The Conscious Person's Guide to Relationships*. This book is really excellent, one of the resources we use in our work. Ken Keyes shares our belief that other people in our lives act as a mirror for what we are accepting and rejecting in ourselves.

Keyes also has a wonderful definition of love that is something like this: " 'I love you' " means that when I'm with you I connect with the loving, lovable, and beautiful parts of myself." In other words, you bring out the best in me and I love that version of myself.

Ken Keyes also works to help people let go of addictive behavior, feeling as he does that you bring all of your addictions with you to a relationship. So when you fall in love you have to look clearly to see if you will be able to put up with the other person's addictions, and vice versa. Why not just get rid of as many as possible?

TWELVE-STEP PROGRAMS

The Twelve-Step programs are based on the Alcoholics Anonymous system of twelve steps to overcoming the disease of addiction.

Many adults today were raised in dysfunctional families; there were either alcohol addictions or other addictive behavior in some way. Children of dysfunctional families find as they grow up that they have a very difficult time creating healthy, loving relationships.

Adult Children of Alcoholics, Alcoholics Anonymous, Cocaine Anonymous, Overeaters Anonymous, and many other groups meet on a regular basis in most major cities in this country. Their various twelve-step programs are very popular, as more and more Americans are letting go of their addictions and working to change their addictive behavior.

These groups are usually offered free of charge, and can be extremely supportive and helpful. They recognize that it is important to free ourselves of addictions in order to have conscious, loving, and fulfilling relationships.

We have not personally been involved in the twelve-step programs. Both of us have been able to let go of our addictions without a program of this type. But many of our clients and friends are avid supporters of them, and we can see the benefits that these groups bring to the lives of our friends.

JOHN BRADSHAW

In his excellent books *Healing the Shame That Binds Us* and *Home Coming*, John Bradshaw deals with the dysfunctional core issues of shame, denial, and loving the inner child, and the other disorders that face adult children of dysfunctional families. There are valuable insights to be gained in reading these books and attending the author's workshops.

APPENDIX B
Sources

There are several sources of knowledge and inspiration we want to acknowledge. The teachings and attitudes of these places and people have been important to our growth and evolution, and much of the material in this book has its roots in the rich warmth of their loving outreach.

ALOHA SPIRIT

There is a wonderful energy born of volcanic islands, white and black sand beaches, tropical jungles, and misty mountains. It lives in the land, the Aina in Hawaiian, and it is the energy of pure love and life force. This spirited energy is part of the people of these magic islands, in their wisdom and in their hearts.

We have both been drawn to these islands for the love and the energy, the life-style, the magic and mystery. The ancient myths still live; the Hawaiian gods and goddesses still roam the valleys and craters.

The spirit of Aloha, unconditional love, is present here. We have been blessed to receive it, and it is our hope that we can help spread some of it to the rest of the world.

SERGE KAHILI KING

Serge Kahili King is an author and teacher, trained by a Hawaiian Kahuna in the ancient system of Huna. He is the president of an organization called Aloha International, a nonprofit educational corporation whose primary mission is spreading the Aloha Spirit. He travels extensively all over the world giving workshops and lectures and has written several excellent books on spiritual development, Huna, and shamanism. For information contact: Aloha International, P.O. Box 665, Kilauea, Kauai, Hawaii 96754 (808) 826-9097.

THE INSIDE EDGE

This dynamic group was founded by Diana and Paul von Welenetz in 1985. It is the largest and most successful ongoing network of leaders in the fields of healing, transformation, and the human potential movement in California. There are three chapters, currently operating in Beverly Hills, Orange County, and San Diego. Contact: The Inside Edge, P.O. Box 692, Pacific Palisades, California 90272 (213) 281-8933.

TIM PIERING

Tim Piering is an author, hypnotherapist, NLP practitioner, and workshop leader. He has written *Breaking Free to Mental and Financial Independence*, *The Book of Findings*, and *Mastery: A Technology for Excellence and Evolution*. He is the co-leader with partner Conley

Falk of the "Mastery Trainings" held in Santa Barbara, California, several times a year. Contact: Sunwest Publishing, 370 W. Sierra Madre Blvd., Sierra Madre, California 91024 (818) 351-0037.

NEW THOUGHT AND SCIENCE OF MIND

The Church of Religious Science, Science of Mind, and Unity Churches are excellent New Thought institutions that have uplifting messages for all. These churches have a particularly dynamic singles network with lots of classes and activities for single people.

APPENDIX C
Program for Success

Program for Success is the name of our company, which is dedicated to fountaining prosperity and light, inspiration and love. If you are interested in finding out about our workshops ("Finding Each Other" and "Making Love Magic") or our books (*The Treasury of Light: An Anthology of New Age Literature*, edited by Mary Olsen Kelly, *Finding Each Other*, and other relationship books that are in progress), please contact us.

We also have professional audiocassette tapes of all the Guided Journeys available.

For a catalogue of products and workshop schedule, contact: Program for Success, P.O. Box 2124, Pahoa, Hawaii 96778 (808) 966-6720.